C(
Man. _

The Underhanded Mind Control Tactics That All Manipulators Use To Take Control In Personal Relationships

John Mentory

Table of Contents

Introduction

Emotional manipulation is a powerful and potentially deadly fact of life. It is not easy to recognize manipulation taking place. Some people are highly skilled at manipulating the emotions of other people in order to serve their own needs and desires. When this manipulation is carried out in a secretive and subtle way it can be referred to as 'covert'.

When you hear the word covert it might make you think of secretive special operations. In the case of emotional manipulation, this is actually accurate. Covert emotional manipulators are carrying out a secret mission to rob you of your self-esteem, willpower and ability to make decisions that are in your own best interest. Worst of all, you may not know this is even happening. The most skilled emotional manipulators will not only be able to hide their attempts to impact and influence you, but will also be able to make you feel as if you are the person who is behaving badly!

There are many different situations in which covert emotional manipulation can occur. One of the most common and also most serious is within the context of a romantic relationship. If you find yourself romantically involved with an emotionally manipulative individual it can be incredibly serious. People stuck in emotionally manipulative relationships risk a range of serious consequences ranging from losing their self-esteem, emotional well being and sense of reality through to becoming seriously depressed and even suicidal.

A romantic relationship is far from the only scenario in which emotional manipulation can occur. Regular friendships are also fertile ground for emotional manipulators to carry out their schemes and plots. Detecting emotionally manipulative behavior in the context of a friendship can be very hard to do if you don't know what to look out for. Some of the consequences of friendship manipulation can involve a high level of dependency, financial burden and a lack of autonomy on behalf of the person who is the victim of the manipulation.

Sadly, families can also be the stage for emotional manipulation to occur. This can be one of the hardest forms of emotional manipulation to detect because people often don't know where the line exists between helping out a relative and being manipulated by them. When covert emotional manipulation occurs in the context of the family it can lead to a wide range of problems such as financial ruin, the division of families and major bad feeling which can continue for generations.

The professional area of life is another arena for covert emotional manipulators. Everyone who has ever worked in an office or other place of work is aware of the degree of politics, power plays and backstabbing that can take place.

Skilled manipulators will use the fact that people expect a certain amount of game playing to occur as a cover for something far more sinister. Emotional manipulation in the workplace can lead to people acting against their own self interest, committing fraud or even facing sexual harassment.

By this point you are aware that in almost any area of life in which people interact with one another there is the potential for covert emotional manipulation to occur. This does not mean that one should give up hope however. Far from it. By knowing how to recognize situations where manipulation can occur, the type of people who are manipulators and the covert tactics they use, people are able to take the power back from manipulators once and for all.

This book will teach you everything you need to know to recognize, neutralize and fight back against covert emotional manipulation. You will understand the specific weapons and tactics that are used by manipulators to achieve their own selfish ends. You will be given a complete toolkit in order to regain control over your own life and stop anyone from having unfair power over you ever again.

What's more, this book will teach you how you can take your past experience of covert emotional manipulation and use it as a powerful lesson to be learned and benefited from in the future. Nothing is wasted if it is learned from and a past experience of emotional manipulation can become a powerful tool in your life if you know how to use it. This book will teach you everything you need to know.

You have a simple choice. You can ignore this book and the valuable information it contains and go through life at risk of being used by others for their own selfish ends. Or, you can read on, apply the information, and live a happy life that is within your own control. Life is too precious and too valuable to risk throwing away your happiness and enjoyment in order to allow others to get ahead at your expense.

The time to take control is now. A war is being fought between good, honest people and deceptive, covert emotional manipulators. Which side are you on? Will you choose to take control or stand by and let the manipulators win?

Read on. Before it's too late.

Chapter 1: Covert Emotional Manipulation - A Guide To The Threat

So what exactly is covert emotional manipulation? Before we begin to explore the type of people who manipulate you and the various tricks and tactics they use to do so it is important to understand exactly what we mean by the term. It is important to understand exactly what is, and isn't, covert emotional manipulation. In order to do so we will examine all three aspects of the phrase separately.

Covert

Covert refers to the emotional manipulation that takes place being performed in a secretive, subtle or underhanded way. Think of covert manipulators as undercover agents on a mission to rob you of your sanity and happiness. The covert aspect of the emotional manipulation is one of the reasons it is so dangerous.

When we know something or someone is bad for us we know to be careful and have our guard up. Our defenses are raised and we are on the look - out for harm and ways to protect ourselves from it. Covert manipulators take aware this foresight from us. They are wolves in sheep's clothing attempting to appear harmless and benign in order for us to drop our guard.

There is an old Chinese expression that translates roughly as 'Daggers are hidden in smiles'. This refers to the fact that often the most charming, friendly people, at least on the surface, will turn out to be the most dangerous and threatening. This is certainly the case with covert emotional manipulators.

Don't for one second think that an emotionally manipulative person will be obvious or easy to spot. Far from it. It is a cruel and bitter irony that often the people who appear to be the best for us turn out to be the worst. The person who seems like Prince Charming or The Perfect

Girlfriend will often turn out to be the spouse or partner from hell. That best friend who seems to know exactly what to say to you and how and when to say it may well turn out to be the worst thing that ever happened to you. And that powerful ally at work who seems to be your teammate and partner on the road to success could well turn out to be a snake in the grass that sought your downfall all along.

Not all manipulation, or manipulators, are covert. Some people will be obviously trying to influence you or emotionally blackmail you. While these types of people can be harmful they are far less dangerous than covert manipulators. Think of the difference between a poisonous snake that is brightly colored and stands out from its environment and one that is camouflaged and blends in. Both can be deadly. However, the brightly colored snake is one which you know to stay well away from. The camouflaged snake is likely to be overlooked until it is too late and its fangs are sunk into you.

Consider the hidden snake to be the manipulator and this book to be your antidote.

Emotional

Now that we understand exactly what is meant by the 'covert' aspect of emotional manipulation, it is important to consider the emotional side. There are various types of manipulation of which emotional manipulation is but one.

Unlike other types of manipulation, such as physical or financial, emotional manipulation can be harder to spot. It is easy to recognize when someone is being physically abusive as we are likely to feel pain and recognize the situation as one which should not be taking place. Financial manipulation is clear too as it is obvious when someone is not trying to hide the fact they are seeking to financially leach from us. Emotional manipulation, however, is far more subtle and hard to detect.

It is sad but true that many people do not have a clear understanding of their own emotional landscape. We live in a culture and world in which emotional behavior and understanding is not often promoted or supported. If people are unaware of their own emotions and how they impact upon them it can be incredibly difficult to realize when someone is manipulating us emotionally. There are several reasons for this.

One reason why emotional manipulation is so hard to spot is because a skilled manipulator will be able to make the emotional experience of knowing them one which is not straightforward. If we were emotionally manipulated in a way which only felt bad all of the time then it would be difficult for the emotional manipulation to continue for a prolonged period of time. The best emotional manipulators know this and so act in a way which makes the experience emotionally confusing for the person involved.

Emotional manipulation is like a drug. It can feel good at first but over the long term it is likely to destroy the life of the person who is a victim of it. Also like a drug addict, people who are being emotionally manipulated are likely to feel they have control of a situation long after the power has been taken out of their hands.

Think of a person's emotional makeup as like a language. A skilled emotional manipulator will take the time to learn the language of an individual in order to be able to speak directly to them in a way which no one else seems able to. The best manipulators are able to understand a person's motivations, desires and fears and use them to great effect. If each emotion a person experiences is like a string, controlling a different part of their life, then think of an emotional manipulator as the puppet master, pulling on the strings and controlling the person in the way that the manipulator desires.

Manipulation

So what exactly is manipulation? Simply put, it is the process of skillful influence. It is one person exerting influence and control over another in order to benefit their self and not the person that they are manipulating.

There are many, many different ways that a person can be manipulated. Some tactics make a person feel that they are acting in their own best interest when in actual fact they are doing the very opposite. Other types of manipulation leave a person knowing they are doing something bad but they nonetheless feel compelled to do so as a result of feeling bad or guilty as a result of the actions of the manipulator.

The most deadly types of manipulation are subtle and hard to predict. Some manipulators are masters of mixing out and out manipulation with behavior that may seem kind, generous and selfless. This is intended to confuse the person who is being manipulated and override their defense mechanisms.

Any situation where a person is being influenced by another to act in a way that benefits the influencer can be counted as manipulation. Of all the types of manipulation in existence, covert manipulation is the most deadly and serious. This is because it can often happen undetected, like a cancerous tumor that is growing inside a person without their knowledge. The emotional nature of the control being exerted means that it impacts upon every aspect of a person's life including their self-esteem, sanity and self-confidence.

Now that you have an overview of the basic concept of covert emotional manipulation it is time to delve deeper. We will explore the types of people who manipulate others and the specific tactics they use to do so. This information could save your life.

Chapter 2: The Wolves in Sheep's Clothing - Recognizing The Manipulators

Understanding what we mean by covert emotional manipulation is not enough to stop it from taking place. Think about serial killers as an example. Understanding what we mean by serial killing is only one piece of the puzzle. It is also necessary to understand the people carrying out the action. The serial killers themselves. The emotional manipulators.

The general characteristics of an emotional manipulator will first be explored before specific types of manipulators are detailed. There are some basic traits and characteristics that most emotionally manipulative people have in common. These general traits can then take specific forms depending on the situation. For example, manipulators acting in the context of a relationship come in various types, as do family manipulators, friendship manipulators and so on.

Think of this section of the book as a guide to spotting various diseases. Only by knowing the warning signs of any given illness can we make an accurate diagnosis and know the corrective remedy to neutralize the threat. This comparison is accurate as emotional manipulation can be a bigger threat to your life than any disease in the world today.

Personality Profile

There are some things that many, although not all, emotionally manipulative people have in common. By being able to recognize and understand the general personality of this type of person you will then be able to narrow them down into a specific type of manipulator. Think of the general traits as the red flags that should alert you to the fact that someone is not right. Once your warning sirens are sounding you are then able to identify the specific threat and counter it.

Superficial Charm

If you expect emotionally manipulative people to come across as unfriendly, cold or evil you are very, very wrong. Quite the opposite is true. Many emotionally manipulative people will, at first, seem like the friendliest, nicest people on the planet. There is a reason for this. If upon meeting someone you decided that they were an unfriendly or otherwise unlikeable person then you would be closed off to them. You would not want to spend any time with them or listen to what they have to say. In order for someone to be emotionally manipulated they must first be willing to open their heart and mind to the actions and words of another. Superficial charm is one way in which manipulators ensure their victims' compliance.

So what do we mean by superficial charm? Simply put, this means that a person comes across as likeable and pleasant on a surface level. This is likely to take the form of both words and deeds. For example, a superficially charming person will often be friendly, positive and energetic at the start. They will use techniques such as friendly personal nicknames to create a false sense of kinship with another. They are likely to be smiling and well presented. Sometimes the charm will ring a little hollow and seem slightly off. The best emotional manipulators, however, are indistinguishable from genuinely charming people. They are able to calibrate the type and intensity of their charm to the victim they are manipulating in order to not appear 'too good to be true'.

So how serious is the problem of superficial charm? Very. Many of the world's most notorious serial killers were able to lure their victims into a false sense of security by coming across as nice, sweet people initially. Think of notorious psychopath Ted Bundy. Many people who have encountered him reported that he came across as incredibly attractive and charming. This softened people's logic and reason and allowed Bundy to commit some of the most unspeakable acts this planet has ever known.

Superficial charm is one of the hallmarks of a psychopath. It is as genuine as a robot. Underneath the charm is nothing but a cold, calculating mind rationally assessing how best to get inside a person's head and lower their defenses.

When people genuinely are charming it is because they want to become close to a person and make them feel good. This is the end goal of the behavior. In the case of an emotional manipulator the charm is simply a means to an end, the first stage in an otherwise lengthy process. Think of the superficial charm as the way of infiltrating a person's emotional fortress. Once the charm has taken effect and the defenses have been breached the real destructive behavior begins.

An Inflated Sense of Worth
Another trademark of an emotionally manipulative person is the fact that they see their own self worth as far higher than it should be. While most people are a mixture of confidence and doubt, pride and humbleness, many manipulators view themselves as being of serious importance and value to the world. Narcissism is a common trait for manipulators to have. This involves the manipulator viewing their own value as being far, far higher than the people around them. In the mind of an emotional manipulator, they are the King of the World and everyone else living in it is simply a peasant, lucky to breathe the same air as the manipulator. This outlook is important for the following reason. As emotional manipulators believe that they are of far greater importance than the person they are manipulating, it provides them with the rational justification to

behave in any way they wish to. An example can help to illustrate this idea.

When a person kills an insect that is annoying them, such as a fly or wasp, it is done without guilt. This is due to the fact that the person recognizes that they are an intelligent, sentient being with emotions, logic and other advanced traits. The insect, on the other hand, is a simple creature without feelings or any real value in the world.

In the mind of an emotional manipulator their victim is of no greater worth than a fly would be to a normal person. As the manipulator generally believes they are of far greater intrinsic worth than the person they are manipulating they do not see any problem with what they are doing. In their eyes they are simply a superior being taking control of an insignificant, inferior being. They are the human and the victim is the insect.

A Lack of Empathy

Emotional manipulators are often sociopaths and as such share many of the same personality traits as classic sociopathy. One such trait is a complete lack of empathy or the ability to experience compassion or any genuine emotion at all.

If a normal person acts badly to someone else they will often feel guilt. The actions they have carried out or the words they have spoken will weigh heavily on their conscience. With emotional manipulators this simply does not occur. The emotional manipulator will never reflect upon what they have done and feel bad about it. This is simply not in their programming to do so.

So does this mean that emotional manipulators will never show signs of guilt or care? Far, far from it. Skilled emotional manipulators are able to give the appearance of being deeply caring. For example, when an emotional manipulator has done something that has caused their victim upset or distress, they will often be able to convincingly feign signs of being distraught at what they have done.

Emotional manipulators are the definition of crocodile tears. On the surface they may seem guilty and remorseful. Guess what? This is just another form of manipulation. On the surface they may seem to be incredibly caring and understanding but this compassion runs no deeper than their facial expression. On the inside they are experiencing no guilt whatsoever and are simply considering how to use the show of guilt as yet another way of getting what they want out of someone.

Evasion

So far we have likened emotional manipulators to a poisonous snake. One which is dangerous and hidden. These are by no means the only way that such people are snakelike. Just like snakes, emotional manipulators are slippery and hard to pin down.

One common trait of emotional manipulators is extreme levels of evasiveness. The emotional manipulator will often want the attention and focus of a conversation to be on the victim rather than on their self. This is due to the fact that emotional manipulators often do not wish to reveal any information about their life or personality. What they do reveal is often either false, partially true or true but deployed in a way which is calculated to have influence and effect rather than being a true opening up of the heart and soul.

One way of being able to tell if a person is being evasive in this way is by paying close attention to how they answer personal questions. If a manipulator is being evasive then they will often either change the subject or provide a vague answer.

For example, if an emotional manipulator were to be asked 'Did you get on well with your siblings when you were younger?' they may reply with something like 'About as well as most people'. This is an example of an evasive, generalized, vague answer. The other route they might take is by responding along the lines of 'What a good question, I've always wanted to know that about you, tell me.' This is an example of switching the focus back to the victim with a mixture of flattery and evasion.

When someone is evasive most or all of the time it is usually because their withholding of information is part of their manipulative weaponry.

Inconsistency

As well as simply evading questions that are asked of them, manipulators will often produce elaborate lies which are designed to have an impact upon their victims. For example, if asked about their childhood, the manipulator will often answer completely differently depending on who they are talking to. If they feel that building a sense of rapport with the victim is important in the moment then they may claim to have had a similar experience of their younger years as the victim. This is intended to create a sense of connection with them and bond with them on an artificial level. If, however, the manipulator senses that gaining sympathy will better serve their purpose in the moment then the manipulator is likely to come up with an elaborate sob story designed to tug on the victim's heart strings.

The best manipulators will ensure that they keep track of their lies over time and present a consistent facade to each victim. Sometimes, in spite of the manipulator's best efforts to keep everything controlled and within their grasp, inconsistencies will begin to emerge in their story. Such inconsistencies are a sign that the person is being deceptive which is a serious red flag and sign that emotional manipulation is occurring.

If you need a better idea of what this looks like, think of Heath Ledger's portrayal of The Joker in the movie The Dark Knight. His infamous question 'Want to know how I got these scars?' is repeated during the movie. Each time, the sociopathic villain gives a different explanation as to how he became disfigured. The truth is never clear. If you have someone in your life who is wildly inconsistent then it may well be a warning sign you have stumbled across a sociopathic villain of your own.

Chapter 3: Kind Cupid or Covert Cobra? - The Romantic Manipulators

The general traits of a manipulator have now been explained. Knowing these is a valuable first step in your fight back against emotional manipulation. The general traits are not enough to protect you fully though. It is important to understand that being able to recognize the general traits is like being able to recognize that you are feeling unwell. That recognition is important but is only a first step. Once you know something is wrong it is important to narrow it down. Knowing the specific types of manipulator that you could come across in life is the next stage in protecting yourself from emotional manipulation.

The first type of emotional manipulator you will be taught to recognize is the romantic manipulator. This is because romantic manipulation is one of the most powerful and deadly forms of covert emotional manipulation that can occur. Tragically, countless people lose their lives each year as a result of being in a relationship with an abusive and emotionally manipulative partner. This can take the form of either physical abuse resulting in death or suicide as a desperate way out from the abuse that has taken place. Romantic manipulators come in various guises and these will now be explored for your protection.

Catfish

Let's start with one of the most well known type of emotional manipulator operating in the world today. The Catfish. Most people are familiar with the antics of the Catfish through portrayals on TV shows or the movie so that they have some idea of the danger that the Catfish presents. Despite this, countless people become victims of the Catfish each and every day. Read on to learn how to avoid becoming the next victim.

A Catfish can be defined as someone who poses as another online in order to ensnare a victim into a romantic relationship. The motivations for doing this are varied. Some people are bored and simply engage in this behavior as a distraction and diversion from their boredom. Other people are lonely and feel that pretending to be someone else is the only way that they will ever feel a connection. Other people are more sinister in their intentions. Some people go into this type of situation looking to emotionally and financially exploit another human being for their own gain.

There are several telltale signs that a Catfish may be at work. Firstly, they are often incredibly reluctant to video chat with their victim or meet them in person. This is due to the fact that they are often using a picture that does not look like them. By video chatting or meeting in person their cover would be blown so this is often avoided. The excuses a person will give for being unable to meet or video chat are often fantastical to the point of sounding almost too elaborate to be true. Catfish over the years have claimed to have been imprisoned, kidnapped or mysteriously ill whenever a victim wishes to speak to them in person or via video!

Another red flag with regards to Catfish is the likelihood that their online profiles on social media seem a little off. For example, a Catfish will often have a limited amount of pictures on their profile. Many victims have only seen one or two pictures of the person they are speaking with. This is due to the fact that they are often taken from another person's social media profile. In order to check this it is always worth performing an image search to see if the picture that the person is using shows up on another social media profile under a different name.

If you suspect you are dealing with a Catfish there are a few key things to remember. Firstly, do not give away any personal information whatsoever, because you don't want to be stalked by the Catfish. It is therefore vital that you do not give away your address or even the general area in which you live. Your place of work or school is another detail of your personal life which should remain private.

Another key to dealing with a Catfish is to avoid providing them with gifts or financial support of any type. Many Catfish are playing their game purely for their own benefit and seeking out material reward for doing so. This is a pitfall that you absolutely must avoid. Many Catfish will also have a carefully worked out story designed to tug on a person's heartstrings to entice them into providing financial support.

Some of the most common ways in which a Catfish will seek to gain this type of provision is by claiming that they are in a bad situation such as being unable to feed himself or pay their bills. Avoid succumbing to the temptation to help. A small request will usually snowball into a larger and larger request and giving in even once shows you are easy to manipulate and will succumb given the right circumstances.

Leeches

A leech gets their name from the bloodsucking creature. Human leeches are even more disgusting than this. They are the equivalent of vampires who exist only to feed on others. There are several types of leeches that you may come across in the context of emotional manipulation within romance.

The first type of leech is the financial leech. This is someone who does not ever contribute towards the payment of anything and expects the person they are romantically involved with to pay for everything. This may start off on a small scale, such as claiming that they forgot their wallet to pay for a dinner or something else that is relatively insignificant in the bigger picture. By doing this, however, the financial leech is covertly manipulating their victim into becoming accustomed to taking financial care of them. The requests will grow over time until the victim is covering almost all of the leeches' expenses. The best financial leeches will do this so gradually that the victim will not know something is amiss until it is too late. Think of the lobster that is killed by gradually heating the water. They are unaware of what is happening to them due to how gradually it occurs. The victims of financial leeches often end up bankrupt due to how thoroughly they have been manipulated.

Cheats

Infidelity in the context of a romantic relationship is an incredibly common occurrence. It is important to note that cheating can occur without covert emotional manipulation. Sometimes people get drunk or make a one off mistake. This is not the type of cheat that we are discussing here. This section refers only to the type of cheats who enter into relationships without the intention of ever remaining faithful. For such people cheating is as natural to them as breathing.

So what are the signs that someone is being cheated on by a covert emotional manipulator? Firstly, the manipulator is likely to be very protective of their personal belongings. This is due to the fact that they will often be in inappropriate contact with many other people at the same time. A classic manifestation of this is the person who keeps their phone facing down at all times in case something incriminating appears on its screen. Some cheats take this to extreme levels and actually have multiple phones or sim cards. Discovering that a romantic partner is keeping a secret mobile phone is a clear sign that something is going very wrong in the relationship.

Another sign of dating a cheat is that the person is very evasive about where they are or who they will be with. A classic type of this behavior is when your cheating partner is claiming to be at work when they are not. Unexplained spending can also be a sign that a cheat is in your life.

Finding receipts for purchases that do not make sense or finding the person spending more money than makes sense are indications that something is amiss.

The type of emotional manipulator that tends to cheat on their victims is often incredibly skilled at making this behavior seem to be the fault of the victim. For example, cheats are often able to place the blame on their victim by pointing out some type of personality flaw or other reason why the manipulator feels cheating on their target is justified.

Bigamists

Bigamy is the practice of having multiple wives. It is widely illegal. Many people over the years have been horrified when a person shows up in their life claiming to be married to their spouse. Similarly as to the case of cheats, bigamists are often able to shift the blame for their behavior away from themselves and their own actions and onto their victim.

One common way in which bigamists are able to covertly manipulate their victims is by claiming they never said they did not have another spouse. On the surface, this sounds absurd, but it is often said in a way which makes it sound like a valid explanation. This is an example of a tactic that is known as 'lying by omission', something that will be explored in greater detail in a later section of this book. Rather than lying by saying something untrue, the bigamist often chooses to lie by not saying an important truth, namely that they have other spouses.

There is one good aspect of discovering a bigamist. Unlike many other types of emotional manipulation, bigamy is against the law. It is therefore possible to seek legal recourse if you discover that bigamy is occurring. Of course, the main challenge is that many bigamists are skilled emotional manipulators to the point that they are able to make the victim feel as if they are the ones in the wrong for reporting the illegal behavior!

Violent Abusers

Of all the types of romantic emotional manipulation that can occur, violent abuse is perhaps the most serious. Sadly, countless incidents of violence and rape occur around the world each and every day. Violent abuse not only wreaks havoc upon a person's body but also upon their mental wellbeing. Thinking that violent abuse is not emotional is missing the point entirely. Violent abuse has a serious emotional impact upon the person suffering it. The ways in which a violent abuser can be identified will now be explored.

Sometimes romantic partners are violently abusive without being manipulative. They may simply have an anger problem and lose their temper. While this is utterly unacceptable it is not the focus of this section. Rather, the type of violent abuse that occurs in conjunction with deliberate emotional manipulation will be explained.

One trademark tactic of a violent abuser is blaming the victim for what has occurred. A common mantra repeated by such sick individuals is 'You made me do it' or 'This was your fault'. For example, if a man is incredibly jealous and hits his girlfriend as a result of this jealousy, he may be able to convince her that she is responsible for making him jealous and is therefore culpable for her own injury.

Another tactic that is frequently employed by violent abusers is denying the reality of what has happened. If a victim points out the physical sign of injury then the manipulator will often deny that they are the one who has caused the problem. They will claim that the victim has fallen or hurt themselves in some other way. Other types of manipulative violent abuser will claim that they accidently caused the injury. "I held your hand a little too tight" or "I just meant to walk past you" are some common types of excuses that are used to explain away physical injury.

Another aspect of covert emotional manipulation that can occur within a violently abusive situation is blackmail. A violent emotional abuser will often claim that they will carry out some act of revenge on their victim should they tell someone what is happening. Some common examples of this include threatening to kill the victim or their loved ones or other more insidious forms of revenge such as leaking sexual photographs or videos onto the internet or to their colleagues. Often, these threats lead to serious mental torment on the part of the victim and create a psychological prison in which they are trapped, and condemned to suffer violent abuse as a result of their fear of the consequences.

Frauds

Frauds are some of the most extreme romantic manipulators in the world. While most emotional manipulators will use deception as part of their range of tactics, frauds are nothing but deception. Their identity, background and everything about them is literally a lie.

Frauds claim to have a different name, age, hometown and back story to that which is actually true. Chillingly, some actually are able to convince themselves that they are telling the truth. Someone who is using a fraudulent identity is likely to have done so before. Cautionary tales exist of men who have used a string of different identities over the years in order to deceive the people they enter into emotional relationships with.

Some of the endgames of frauds include making personal financial gain from the relationships they enter into. Some examples of this include taking out joint bank accounts and disappearing with the money. They also are known to get their fraudulent identity onto the title of property, use it as collateral to take out large loans and then disappear without being heard from again.

The victims of frauds are manipulated in two key ways and suffer two significant corresponding losses. Not only do fraud victims lose the person they thought they loved but they lose financially as well. The loss of a relationship with a fraud can be emotionally confusing and devastating for victims. They feel a mixture of hurt, confusion, anger and loss. Not only do fraud victims lose their relationship but they also find out the person they loved never even existed. This can cause severe mental health issues ranging from trust issues all the way to questioning reality and a loss of sanity in extreme but not rare cases.

Combinations
The above types of romantic emotional manipulators are by no means the only types that exist. They are, however, the main archetypes of emotional romantic manipulation

and are therefore vital to look out for and be aware of.

Often, a covert emotional manipulator will fall into several of the above categories, either at once, or displaying different types of emotional manipulation at different times. For example, a fraud may also be a violent abuser and a cheat.

If you find out that someone you know falls into one of the above categories then be extra vigilant regarding the others. For example, if someone cheats on you, then they may well be exploiting you in some other way. This is something to be very aware of.

Chapter 4: Friend or Frienemy?

Covert emotional manipulation can occur within the boundaries of relationships that are friendly rather than romantic. This is often harder to detect because we sometimes pay less attention to friends than we do to romantic partners. Just as there are various types of relationship manipulators there are also various types of friendship manipulators. The main types of emotional manipulators that operate within the context of a so called 'friendship' will now be explored.

Two Faces

This type of emotional manipulation may sound petty but it's not. 'He is so two faced!' may sound like the complaint of a high school student but it is in fact a very serious type of manipulation which can have dire consequences upon a person's life.

A two faced friend can be defined as someone who acts one way around a person and another way behind their back. Not all examples of two faced behavior are the work of a covert emotional manipulator but many are. The key difference between manipulative and non-manipulative two faced behavior is that, in the case of manipulation, the two faced behavior is carried out with the intention of benefiting the person who is being two faced at the expense of the victim.

So what are some common signs of someone being two faced and manipulative? One key warning is when people seem to be keen to spend time with someone but only alone and not in the company of a wider social circle. The manipulator will always try and strive for this to occur as it allows them to be one way to a person and another way when they are not around. If the person was forced to interact with their victim around others then inconsistencies in their attitude would become apparent.

A two faced manipulator can impact upon a victim's life severely. For example, interacting with a two faced person can cause a person to have severe trust issues in the long run. They may also suffer from paranoia, panic, anxiety and other mental health issues.

Often, a two faced manipulator will gain a victim's trust and get their victim to open up to them about their life and the people in it. The victim will do so, having being lulled into a false sense of security that the manipulator is someone they trust and can have faith in. The manipulator will then use the privileged information that has been confided in them against their 'friend' in order to cause division and doubt among the other people in their life. Every word that the victim speaks to a two faced manipulator can potentially be used as a weapon to hurt them in the future.

Leeches

Friendship leeches are somewhat similar to romantic leeches, with a few key differences. Whereas romantic leeches are known for charming their victims before taking financial advantage of them, friendship leeches act more gradually, less severely and typically over a longer period of time.

Some of the key warning signs that a friend is leeching from you are as follows. They never volunteer to contribute towards the payment of anything, even if it directly benefits them. For example, if you go out to grab a bite together, they will just expect you to pay for the meal without even saying anything. If pressed, they will claim to have forgotten their credit card, be short on cash, or 'You get this one and I'll get the next", an offer of repayment which of course never gets made.

One of the ways in which friendship leeches are able to covertly manipulate the friend into providing them is by playing on the friend's emotional weaknesses, whatever they may be. For example, if the friend is from a privileged background, the manipulator will emphasize how lucky the friend is in comparison to their own background. This will then be used against the friend as a form of guilt tripping in order to ensure that their friend takes care of their financial requirements.

Friendship leeches can also exist in a non-financial form. Some examples of this include always expecting the one that is being manipulated to put their self out on a limb while the manipulator is never willing to do so. For example, the person that is being emotionally manipulated may be expected to only go to the places that the manipulator wishes to go to and never the places that they desire. The manipulator may also expect the friendship to run on their terms, such as by only communicating when the manipulator desires.

Friendship leeches can be harder to spot due to the lesser severity of their actions. It can be hard to draw the line between a genuine leech and someone who is just behaving unconsciously inconsiderately. A useful way of making the distinction between the two types of people is by drawing the person's attention to their behavior. A manipulator may feign concern and regret but they will be unable to make any meaningful change in the long run whereas someone who was not intentionally manipulating the other will be able to change.

Bullies

Bullying is far from something that only happens at school. Bullies can be found in any walk of life, including friendship. Bullying between friends can have very destructive effects due to the covert nature of this type of manipulation. Some examples will now be provided.

One of the reasons that bullying is so covert when carried out in the context of friendship is it is often justified as being playful or teasing. Watch any movie involving a group of friends and you will typically see some harsh jokes tossed around and fun being made at the expense of others. This is not bullying.

Bullying occurs within the context of friendship when there is an intention of hurting or causing distress to the other person. When a group of friends are merely joking around then their attention is only to have fun with one another and not to cause any harm. The line has been crossed into bullying when the manipulator has not got any positive intentions behind their words and actions. They may mask their behavior as fun and friendly but in reality is anything but.

So what are the consequences of bullying? This type of covert manipulation can erode the self-belief and confidence of an individual. If, for example, their manipulator subtly makes comments regarding their intelligence, the person may begin to subconsciously agree with their bully.

Another potential impact that manipulative bullying can have is causing the victim to take out their anger and hurt on someone else. It is often said that if someone is bullied they learn to do the same to others. If a manipulator manages to upset someone then it is possible that the person they have hurt will repeat their behavior, usually unintentionally, in the future.

So how can we tell if bullying is occurring or if it is simply friendly friendship banter? True friends will stop or dial down any behavior that they see is having a genuine negative impact upon someone. A manipulator, on the other hand, will not. They may give the appearance of caring but often they will simply begin to hurt the other person in a more subtle and less obvious way. A bully will also tend to react badly to any comments being made about them, whereas friends will often be able to take and enjoy the same level of joking and playing around that they show to their friends.

Predators

Predators are those who wish to find and prey upon weaker individuals in order to exploit them for their own gain. This is a particularly dangerous type of covert manipulation due to the fact that it involves people who are in a vulnerable state. Some of the types of people that predators look for are those who have experienced a major life change such as a divorce or bereavement, people who are mentally ill or have learning difficulties, addicts and recovering addicts and other types of people susceptible to manipulation.

A predator will begin by being kind and friendly to a target in a way that they feel they will be particularly receptive to. This often involves over the top displays of friendship and intense emotional bonding and support in order to win over the trust of the predator's target. The most highly skilled predators will seek out people who have something missing in their life and aim to fill the gap. For example, if someone does not have many friends who they can open up to, then the predator will aim to become that person. In this way, the predator makes the victim reliant upon them.

Once the predator has gained the trust of their vulnerable target they will typically begin to start extracting money and other favors from the victim. This often starts in a small way and builds gradually over time. This incremental approach is used in order to allow the predator to make the victim used to providing for them in a way which is not overwhelming at first. If the victim refuses to comply with the wishes of the predator then the predator will typically withdraw whatever emotional role they were providing in the victim's life. This leaves a void which the victim desperately wishes to fill, often complying with the wishes of the predator in the process.

Ideological Manipulators

Ideological manipulators are some of the most dangerous types within the area of friendship. This is due to the fact that an ideological manipulator is not only motivated by their desire to control and influence another human being, although this is certainly a key driver for them. What separates ideological manipulators from other types is the fact that they have a cause or higher purpose driving their manipulation. When combined with the sociopathic personality that is so common to manipulators it makes for a potentially deadly combination.

So what exactly is an ideological manipulator? This is someone who attempts to recruit or convert someone to an ideology or cause under the guise of genuine friendship. Some examples include cult members who befriend potential recruits and terrorists who groom vulnerable people to fight for and join their cause. The ideological manipulator is dangerous as they will have often been trained in grooming methods by their ideology which is intended to exploit the psychology of people in order to lure them to the cause.

The process of ideological manipulation typically works as follows. The manipulator will begin by seeking to get to know the target in as much detail as possible. This allows for weaknesses and vulnerabilities to be spotted which can be exploited later. It is common for manipulators of this type to supply their target with gifts and other types of material favor. This is intended to create a sense of debt and owing towards the manipulator. The manipulator will slowly, over time, begin to introduce their ideology. This often starts in quite a casual and non-threatening way. Any controversial or dangerous aspects of the ideology will be hidden until much later.

The consequences of falling prey to an ideological manipulator can be severe. Sadly, many young people from around the world have decided to join terrorist causes after being brainwashed by their skilled recruiters. This is a genuine example of a type of friendship manipulation which can end in a loss of life, not only of the target, but of innocent people at the hand of the target.

Chapter 5: Office Politics or Sociopathic Tricks? - The Workplace Manipulators

The workplace is a fertile ground for manipulation of various types to occur. Many people will find they encounter at least several of the following types of workplace manipulators over the course of their career. It can be hard to know how to draw the line between normal workplace politics, gossip and banter and actual manipulation. By being able to identify some of the main types of manipulators that exist within the world of work it can help potential targets to stay away from the wrong type of colleague before they find their world has been turned upside down and their professional life damaged beyond repair.

The Blackmailer
The Blackmailer is a type of workplace manipulator that can have a serious impact not only on their victims' careers but also on their

mental wellbeing and overall sanity. The basic method of the blackmailer is to appear friendly and highly trustworthy at first. This is usually achieved by finding a newcomer to the workplace or someone who does not fit in with others particularly well.

Once a suitable target has been identified the blackmailer will invest a serious amount of time and effort in winning over their target and deceptively earning their trust. This is often done by taking a new member of staff under their wing and offering to mentor them and make their new life at the company as easy as possible.

The blackmailer will often form a friendship with their intended target that occurs outside of work as well as inside work. This is essential as for the blackmailer's manipulation to be effective it must involve the target seeing the blackmailer more as a trusted friend than simply as a colleague.

Over time, the blackmailer will begin to subtly elicit sensitive information from their target. This could involve controversial opinions about the other people that the two work with or even sensitive details of the victim's personal life such as their sexual orientation or political views. The blackmailer will keep going until they feel they have accumulated a sufficient amount of information to use against their victim.

Once the blackmailer has some powerful information to hold against their target, such as a covert phone recording of them saying something disparaging, or a photograph of the target behaving controversially in some way, the blackmailer will begin to hold it against them. They may make threats such as planning to reveal the sensitive information to others within the workplace or even the target's loved ones and family.

The blackmailer will often demand increasing levels of money or favors from the victim in order to keep their secrets safe. The victim ends up living in a constant state of fear as they do not know when and if they will have their secrets revealed. This has a destructive effect on the victim's mental health and can lead to breakdowns and major levels of anxiety.

The False Ally

The false ally is a type of workplace manipulator who is skilled at hiding their true intentions. They will seem to be a keen ally of their target. They are likely to suggest to their target that together they will go big places in the workplace and support each other's climb up the career ladder.

The false ally will often begin by making an over the top show of helping out their intended target. This is designed to ensure that the target sees them as a trustworthy figure and also feels a debt of gratitude towards the false ally. Once the false ally feels they have earned the trust and respect of their target they will begin to exert subtle levels of control over them.

Some typical plays in the playbook of the false ally include coercing a victim into acting in the self-interest of the ally and not of the victim. This will usually take place under the guise of doing 'what's best for both of us' when in actual fact it will be anything but. This type of manipulation is especially effective if the victim is naive and idealistic. The false ally is able to tap into the desires and ambitions of the victim in order to gain their compliance in carrying out the false ally's bidding.

The endgame of the false ally is typically to see their own career advance while their target's either stalls or is damaged irreparably. This often takes the form of the false ally gaining some form of recognition, like a promotion, at the expense of the target, but due to the efforts and choices the target has been coerced into. Often, the victim has no idea that they have been played like a puppet until it is too late and the false ally has already benefited.

The Abuser of Power

It is a well known fact that power has the potential to corrupt human beings. The workplace is one of the most common arenas for such behavior to occur. The abuse of power can take many different forms but they all involve someone unfairly wielding a position of hierarchical authority over another person.

Some common examples of abuses of power include those in supervisory or management positions asking for inappropriate or over the top levels of support and compliance from those they have power over. This can take less serious forms, such as getting workers to put in hours that they are not paid for or take more serious forms such as pressuring female employees into sexual liaisons in exchange for the promise of promotions and job security.

It is important to draw a distinction between someone who exerts power in a legitimate fashion and someone who abuses it. In order for the wielding of power to cross the line into the realms of covert emotional manipulation it must fulfill the following criteria. Firstly, the manipulator must have a position of authority over their target, such as by being their manager or some other formal position of authority. Secondly, the manipulator must use their power in a way which is intended to control their victim through the manipulation of their emotions. Abusers of power can draw on aspects such as their victim's feelings of job insecurity or doubt about their future.

Abusers of power are particularly dangerous types of manipulators as they have very little chance of being caught. This is due to the fact that it can be difficult for someone within a workplace to blame their boss or superior for their own actions. Unless clear evidence exists, which it very rarely does, then it is likely to come down to the word of the victim against the word of the manipulator. Sadly, this is rarely sufficient evidence for a company to take any kind of action against the person who has abused the power they hold.

The Sexual Predator
Sexual predators can take the form of almost any other type of workplace manipulator but also exist on their own. Simply put, a sexual predator is one who seeks to act in an inappropriate sexual way towards someone they work with. This can range in severity.

At one end of the scale, workplace sexual predators may simply make another member of staff feel uncomfortable. This can be through looks, gestures or inappropriate physical contact. Despite this being the most mild type of sexual predatory behavior that can occur, it is still incredibly serious and should be avoided at all costs.

Sadly, many workplace sexual predators take things a lot further than merely making a victim feel uncomfortable. Many sexual predators will coerce their victim into carrying out behaviors of a sexual nature that they feel pressured or forced into doing. In order to ensure that their victim stays quiet about what has occurred, the predator will often gather some kind of compromising evidence, such as photographs, which the predator threatens to expose to the victim's colleagues and family should they cause any problems for the predator.

Although many workplaces have policies in place which are intended to protect against any type of inappropriate sexual behavior in the workplace they are rarely enough to stop the worst predators from going about their manipulation. This is due to the fact that skilled predators of this nature are able to ensure they do not leave any evidence whatsoever. They are also likely to choose victims who have low self-esteem or have some other reason that makes them unlikely to tell others of what has taken place.

The Bully

Bullies may seem to be a fairly trivial type of workplace manipulator but this is far from the case. Bullying can have a severe impact upon someone's happiness and wellbeing and is often hard to detect and even harder to stop. This is due to the fact that a skilled manipulator engaged in the practice of bullying is likely to mask their actions as friendship or advice. Underneath the friendly veneer, however, something far more dangerous and sinister is occurring.

Bullying can range in severity. On one end of the scale, a bully may seem to be making jokes that just happen to involve the victim. However, this is not what is happening. What seems like a joke is often actually an attempt to gradually erode the victim's confidence and leave them vulnerable and doubtful. A cognitive dissonance is created in the victim's mind as on the one hand they are aware that the comments or actions of the bully are hurting them but on the other they do not want to appear overly sensitive or thin skinned. This often results in the victim begrudgingly accepting the bullying that is taking place, even if it is hurting them in the long run.

In order for bullying to work the manipulator chooses their target carefully. They are likely to select someone who lacks self-confidence and is not particularly popular within the workplace. This is due to the fact that the victim will put up with the bullying as it is often the only form of attention they have received in the workplace up until that point.

Bullying can have severe consequences in the long run. It can chip away at the victim's confidence and happiness and, perversely, create a sense of dependency on the manipulator and the attention they provide. The effects can be with a victim for the rest of their life. They may have severe difficulty in trusting another again and forming any type of healthy relationship in the future. This is due to the fact they will have fallen into the pattern of seeking approval and validation via negative attention.

Chapter 6: Family Drama or Covert Kinship Manipulation?

Family covert manipulation is one of the most difficult and potentially painful areas in which manipulation can occur. This is due to the fact that people are likely to feel a deeper bond and connection with their family members than they are in the case of friends or colleagues. Our love and sense of loyalty for our relatives can lead to us being blind to when they are covertly manipulating our emotions. One of the most difficult things to determine is whether a family member is being covertly manipulative or simply being a normal, dramatic, member of the family. By exploring the main types of family manipulators you can protect yourself against manipulation where it hurts the most.

The Victim
The victim is one of the hardest types of family manipulator to deal with. This is due to the fact that the victim is likely to present an emotionally

appealing sob story that has been tweaked and engineered to tug upon the target's heart strings. The victim sees their life as an unfair and unlucky one. They are likely to find a family member who has experienced success and hold this against them. Some of the ways in which victims operate will now be detailed.

One of the most common areas for a victim manipulator to act is within the context of a sibling relationship. Often, the victim will portray themselves as the unfortunate, unloved and uncared for member of their family. They will take every opportunity to emphasize how they have never had a fair shot in life and how their parents never gave them the love, attention and opportunity that another sibling had.

The most effective victims are those who manage to incorporate a grain of truth into their story. This grain of truth will be exaggerated severely but because there is an element of truth to what their saying their manipulation is likely to be more effective. Victims will often seek to extract money and other forms of support from members of the family that they are able to guilt trip.

As to whether the victim believes the story they are telling, it depends on the circumstance. Some victims are consciously aware of the ways in which they are exaggerating and distorting the truth whereas others act almost instinctively, doing whatever happens to work in their pursuit of control and support from another member of the family. One thing that almost all victim type manipulators have in common, however, is their deeply held belief that their actions are justified, that they are righting some kind of wrong that destiny has dealt them. This sense of conviction and justice is a dangerous thing as it can inspire the manipulator to cross each and every line in pursuit of getting what they want.

The Controller

Controlling relatives are common to every family. It is rare to find a family situation which does not feature some kind of overbearing or overprotective parent, uncle or sibling. Not every relative who is controlling in some way is a covert emotional manipulator. Those who are though are dangerous indeed as their behavior is often seen as normal and therefore acceptable. The key distinction that must be drawn is that while some people are naturally controlling, controlling manipulators actively seek to control through the deliberate manipulation of another's emotions.

Some examples of the type of controlling behavior which crosses the line into covert manipulation includes when a family member does not respect the privacy of one of their relatives and goes through deeply personal data such as their bank statements or social media profiles in order to gain some information that can be used as leverage. Such behavior is often explained away as being caring, compassionate or somehow in the best interests of the victim. In reality, it is anything but.

Because of the emotional intimacy and familiarity that many families have with one another, controllers will often have a detailed understanding of exactly which buttons to press in order to get their target to behave in the way they want. Over the years of knowing the victim they have built up a thorough picture and understanding of exactly what drives and motivates them.

For example, if a relative who wishes to covertly manipulate the emotions of another knows that their intended victim is sensitive to criticism then the manipulator may subtly and persistently criticize a victim into complying with their wishes. When the victim does as the manipulator wishes, the criticism is withdrawn. When the victim does not do as the manipulator wishes, the criticism continues. This system of punishment and 'reward' conditions the victim into becoming compliant and weak willed. It should be noted that the mere absence of a negative behavior is the best that this type of manipulator has to offer.

Some of the common aspects of a person that family manipulators of this type seek to control include the financial decisions of the person they are controlling, their choice of partner or spouse, their career choices and even their personal appearance. Some manipulators of this type operate under the misguided belief that they are behaving in the victim's best interests while others harbor no such illusion and merely do it to exert power and for their own amusement.

The Divider

The divider is one of the most insidious and dangerous types of covert emotional manipulator. This is due to the fact that the type of manipulation they carry out will often be entirely under the radar. The divider's mission is simple - to create mistrust, division and suspicion between members of the same family.

One of the favorite tactics of the divider is to subtly play two members of the same family off against one another. The divider will be in the middle of the two, always appearing to favor and be on the side of whoever they are talking to at the time. One of the hallmarks of this type of manipulation is it rarely comes across as an obvious attempt at eroding the bonds of family. Rather, the divider will often come across as someone who is simply sharing information or looking out for particular members of the family.

Is everyone who causes division in a family a covert emotional manipulator? No, definitely not. Dividers are those individuals who have the intention of causing division. Many people cause division unintentionally or carelessly. This does not apply to the divider. The divider sets out with the clear intention and aim of tearing people apart from one another.

So what motivates the divider? It is often a fear of change and a desire to control. If a divider feels that the established structure of a family is changing, such as by previously distant relatives becoming closer, the divider will often seek to meddle until the status quo is ignored.

Another common motivation for dividers is to ensure that they will not lose out on any power structures that form within a family. Dividers often have a very tactical view of a family. Whereas as psychologically healthy people will view a family as a collection of related individuals with various degrees of closeness, a divider will envision a family as a complex web of power involving alliances, enemies and hierarchies and sub-hierarchies. By keeping members of the family from becoming close, the divider ensures they have influence over any given family situation.

One of the keys of dealing with a divider is to never take anything they say at face value. If a divider tells you something about someone else in the family, do not believe them. Verify any claims for yourself. This will help to ensure that you do not become another pawn in their neurotic struggle for power. If you become involved in a divider's schemes you risk not only losing some of the close relationships within your family but also being blamed for the collapse of familial closeness that may well occur following a divider's influence.

Chapter 7: The Manipulator's Playbook - Covert Emotional Manipulation Tactics

So far, we have explored the concept of Covert Emotional Manipulation and also taken an in-depth look at the different situations which are susceptible to manipulators as well as the specific types of manipulators that exist. There is one missing piece of the puzzle in providing you with everything you need to spot a covert emotional manipulator and stop them before they take over and ruin your life.

It is rare that someone is simply going to tell you 'Oh by the way, I'm your boss, and I will be manipulating your emotions by abusing my power'. Instead, it is up to you to recognize the tactics of covert emotional manipulation and when it is occurring.

In this section of the book you will be given a comprehensive insight into the different specific tactics that manipulator's use in the course of their schemes and plots. Each tactic will be explained and examples will be given of when and how it can occur. Finally, you will be given a clear guide on how to resist each specific tactic. Think of this as your armor against the many weapons that the manipulators have stored up ready to use against you.

It is often said that 'knowledge is power'. If this is the case then consider the knowledge you are about to receive a source of ultimate protective power. Understanding the tactics of manipulators, and how to counter them, could make the difference between living a happy life that is in your control or being a puppet in someone else's manipulative master plan.

Love Bombing
What It Is
Love bombing is an incredibly intense opening tactic that is used by different types of manipulators in many different situations. It

involves showering the victim with a non-stop bombardment of positive sentiment, word and action in the initial stages of the interaction between the manipulator and their victim. This is likely to take as many forms as the manipulator can think of. For example, the victim may receive compliments both in person and via digital communication, receive gifts, non-stop positive attention and praise and very warm facial expressions and body language when the manipulator is with them in person.

The theory behind love bombing is it short circuits the rational part of a person's brain. When someone is on the receiving end of a non-stop barrage of positive emotion it can prevent their ability to rationally analyze the situation. This is due to the fact that when a person is showered with non-stop positivity of the type that love bombing involves it leads to an actual biochemical change in the body. If you think of the earliest stages of a genuine romantic relationship, the people involved are not thinking. They are swept away by their positive feelings and the accompanying powerful chemical that are coursing through their bodies.

It is important to note that someone can be very positive without it being a case of manipulation or love bombing. The key difference is that, in the case of love bombing, the manipulator will never say or imply anything negative at all, and the intensity and frequency of the positive interactions will far exceed anything that is considered normal or acceptable by the standards of most people. If someone seems too good to be true then they almost certainly are.

How It Occurs

The love bombing phase of a manipulation usually begins when a manipulator finds someone they feel would be receptive to their efforts. For example, if someone is seeking a person to emotionally manipulate within the context of a romantic relationship, the manipulator may seek them out via online dating, singles bars or other places filled with potential targets.

The manipulator will then screen as to the likely effectiveness of the love bombing technique. Manipulators have no desire to invest their time or efforts into someone who is unlikely to be impacted by the love bombing phase. Ways in which manipulators seek to know in advance whether their love bombing will work include giving just a little bit of positivity and attention to the potential victim. If the victim responds excessively favorably then it is indicative that they will be especially sensitive and vulnerable to a greater, more prolonged and more intense form of positive attention in the future.

The most skilled manipulators will carry out love bombing in a way which does not feel untoward to the victim. The best manipulators are able to portray their personality in a way which makes it seem as if they are a genuinely loving person who is just naturally expressing how they feel rather than making a concerted effort to short circuit their victim's defenses.

Love bombing can occur in almost any scenario - romantic, friendship, workplace or even family. It is most commonly used in a romantic context as this arouses the least suspicion, as our culture puts forward the idea of intense love as something desirable. In the case of friendship it is likely to be slightly less intense and focus more on creating a deep bond between people, which of course will later be exploited.

In the workplace love bombing can take the form of excessive praise and compliments of a member of the workplace's efforts and ideas. Family love bombing can be particularly impactful due to the ability of the manipulator to draw on the cultural idea of family being the most important thing and the natural expectation that family members will have a deep sense of love and connection with one another.

How To Resist

The absolute key to resisting the love bombing tactic is to recognize it early on and stop it before it gets started. This is due to the fact that, if love bombing is allowed to continue for even a short period of time, it can override the victim's ability to think critically and analyze the situation. Spotting this tactic in its early stages is therefore the victim's best chance of dealing with it.

So how exactly does a person spot when love bombing is occurring? There are several ways. Firstly, it is important to take note of any gut feeling or rational voice in the back of your mind. If something seems too good to be true it almost certainly is. Any behavior, even a positive behavior that seems excessive is likely to be suspicious and not what it seems.

Secondly, it is vital to seek the opinion of a trusted person outside of the situation. When we are the ones involved in something it is difficult to impossible to assess it rationally and with our best judgment. By opening up to someone else about what is happening it allows them to analyze the scenario impartially from outside of it. This is particularly effective as love bombing is reliant upon the victim and the manipulator existing within a little bubble that is not penetrable by the outside world. This allows the influence to occur unimpeded. By bringing a third party into the situation it allows for the bubble to be deflated and the manipulation to be stopped before it really begins.

Intermittent Positive Reinforcement

What It Is

Intermittent positive reinforcement is something that usually follows the love bombing stage. If the love bombing phase of a manipulation can be understood as the non-stop blitz of the victim with positivity, praise and intense emotions then the intermittent positive reinforcement phase can be understood as a dialing down of the intensity.

Rather than unconditionally and continually bombarding the victim with praise no matter what they do, as is the case with love bombing, IPR (intermittent positive reinforcement) involves the manipulator rewarding the victim's desired behaviors on an inconsistent basis. For example, if the manipulator wishes for the victim to respond to the manipulator's communications in a rapid manner, then the manipulator will show some positive response when this does occur, but not all of the time.

Let's illustrate the above scenario. Imagine the manipulator texting the victim four times in one day. The victim responds promptly all four times. Three of the times, the manipulator will reward the victim with some kind of praise or other positive response. The fourth time, despite the victim behaving in the same way, there will be no positive reinforcement. This will leave the victim on edge and craving the positive reinforcement which has been withheld.

It is a universal principle of life that living creatures want what they know to be pleasurable but not always obtainable. This is why men will chase women who are difficult to get and why performing animals are only sometimes given food when they jump through a hoop. If something is predictably attainable it loses its desirability. By making positive reinforcement intermittent, the manipulator is ensuring that the victim's desire for it is as strong as possible.

The positive reinforcement itself can take several forms. It can be verbal, such as through spoken praise, or non-verbal, such as through smiling, touching or positive facial expressions. The manipulator will often use the type of reinforcement that the victim responds best to, but also will change it enough to ensure that the victim does not take things for granted or become bored. Keeping the interest levels of the victim high is a key part of the manipulation at this stage.

How It Occurs

The most likely time for IPR to begin is when the victim has been thoroughly softened up by an initial technique such as love bombing. Once a manipulator can tell the victim is beginning to be influenced in the way that has been intended they know they can move on to further stages of the manipulation.

A common occurrence in the initial stages of IPR is for the victim to actually notice that something is amiss without being able to put their finger on exactly what. Sometimes, the victim will question the manipulator as to why they seem inexplicably cold or withdrawn in contrast to their previous levels of non-stop love and attention. The manipulator is sure to use this opportunity to make the victim feel like a demanding, insecure and paranoid individual. By getting inside the victim's head at this stage and making them question what they are thinking and feeling, the manipulator is able to effectively sow the seeds for more intense mind games to be played further down the line.

A common pattern of manipulators is to ease into the process of IPR gradually. So, for example, they will begin by only failing to positively reinforce a desired behavior roughly 10% of the time. They will then gradually increase this percentage over time. This way of carrying out IPR works in the manipulator's favor as it prevents the victim from realizing all of a sudden that something is wrong or changed. It also gives the victim a subtle sense of the manipulator and the positivity they represent slipping away from them. It is human nature to chase after something we feel is slipping away and this chasing is exactly what the manipulator is relying upon.

How To Resist

Resisting IPR can be very difficult as it often follows a defense lowering phase such as love bombing. Just because IPR is difficult to resist, however, it does not mean it is impossible to do so.

Some of the main things to look out for with regards to IPR is someone seeming to go out of their way to praise or ignore a certain behavior, seemingly on a whim. Normal people do not care enough about the behavior of a person to reward it as intensely as a manipulator does. If someone did care that much then they certainly wouldn't withhold their approval from time to time as is the case with IPR. Therefore, an inconsistent attitude to behavioral response from another individual is a red flag that IPR is occurring.

As well as looking out for the actions of the potential manipulator it is vital to keep a close eye on one's own emotions and behaviors as well. If a person finds that they are chasing or craving the approval of another to an extent that feels unnatural, unnerving or too intense then it is a sign that something is wrong. It is important to note that craving the attention of someone does not automatically mean that the person is a manipulator. It is almost always a sign, however, that some kind of emotional imbalance is taking place. By recognizing this it gives the person a chance to take a step back and try and analyze exactly why they feel that way.

If you suspect that IPR is being used against you then the most effective thing you can do is to cease interaction with the person carrying it out immediately. IPR is reliant upon a response from the victim so if no response is provided then IPR cannot continue. People who withdraw their behavioral response in this way may notice that the suspected manipulator reverts to the love bombing technique in an attempt to elicit a response from the victim. If you notice a pattern of love bombing following IPR then it is almost certain you are dealing with a covert emotional manipulator. You need to get out of the relationship and situation ASAP.

Negative Reinforcement

What It Is

Negative reinforcement is the flipside of positive reinforcement. Just as positive reinforcement involves a manipulator 'rewarding' the behavior of an individual, negative reinforcement involves the manipulator 'punishing' behavior that the manipulator sees as undesirable.

Negative reinforcement can take various active or passive forms. Some active forms of negative reinforcement include verbally insulting the victim after they say or do something displeasing, physically hurting the victim, encouraging others to chastise the victim and other similar forms of behavior. Passive negative reinforcement can involve the withdrawal of compliments or other forms of positive reinforcement. Sometimes a manipulator will discover that freezing out their victim and acting cold to them is a very effective form of negative reinforcement. This is particularly the case if the victim has issues with abandonment and acceptance.

Some of the most sadistically sociopathic manipulators use negative reinforcement in a way which is intended to ruin a victim's psyche and emotional balance on a deep level. The manipulator will use negative reinforcement in the predictable way, namely to discourage an unwanted behavior. However, occasionally, the manipulator will use negative reinforcement at random. This creates a sense of utter unpredictability in the mind of the victim. As they do not know when they will receive some form of punishment from the manipulator they exist in a state of terror and dread. This actually produces chemical changes in the body, such as by increasing the production of stress hormones. This makes the victim biologically vulnerable to further manipulative efforts.

How It Occurs
Negative reinforcement often occurs as the third step in a linear three step process, with the first two steps being love bombing followed by IPR.

When negative reinforcement is deployed in this way, as the third step, it is especially effective. This is due to the fact that the victim has already been softened up by the love bombing and made emotionally vulnerable. On top of that, the victim is in a state of emotional neediness and chasing as a result of the IPR. The combination of these two emotional states means that the negative reinforcement is more powerful than it would be without the preceding stages.

One of the reasons why negative reinforcement can be so devastating is because it does not fit congruently with the picture of the manipulator that the victim has built up until this point. Before the negative reinforcement occurs, the victim has seen only intense positivity from the manipulator during the love bombing stage and then a slight lessening of this during the IPR phase. When the manipulator suddenly starts to negatively reinforce it hits the victim extra hard.

The negative reinforcement from the manipulator can be very difficult for the victim to comprehend in a logical fashion. This is due to the fact that it is almost impossible to reconcile the negative, hurtful behaviors from the manipulator with their earlier displays of love and affection. In order to avoid extreme cognitive dissonance from occurring, the victim often rationalizes this new behavior as being something positive and caring, when in reality it is anything but.

Sometimes manipulators will seek to take negative reinforcement a step further and reinforce the exact same behavior positively sometimes and negatively other times. This can create a sense of unpredictable terror for the victim. They are left never knowing what the response of the manipulator will be in any given situation. This is incredibly stressful for the victim. This high level of stress suits the purpose of the manipulator as it stops the victim from being able to think rationally. Instead, the victim exists in a state of moment to moment emotional anxiety and dread.

How To Resist

Resisting negative reinforcement can be incredibly challenging. This is due to the fact that a skilled manipulator will often only move to the negative reinforcement phase once they feel that the victim has become emotionally vulnerable following earlier manipulation techniques such as love bombing and IPR. Because of this it can be hard for the victim to correctly identify that negative reinforcement is taking place. There are some steps however that can be taken to resist this evil practice and regain control of one's own emotional boundaries.

A key question to ask oneself if negative reinforcement is suspected is 'Am I doing something I feel bad about?'. This is a simple but powerful tool in the fight against the manipulator. By choosing to judge behavior through the lens of how the victim feels about it, rather than how the manipulator feels about it, it allows the victim to regain control over their life and play by their own rules rather than the rules of the person manipulating them. The difficulty with this approach is the necessity of being able to take a step back and say 'I suspect negative reinforcement is taking place'.

A key to being able to properly identify negative reinforcement is ensuring that the manipulator is never allowed too much time alone with you. If you can attempt to include others in the process of interaction then it allows for some monitoring and understanding to take place from a third party who is in a position to assess the situation using logic rather than emotion.

If the manipulator is attempting to reinforce negatively through the use of text messages or social media messages then it can be helpful to show these to a trusted friend. The friend will be able to assess them from a detached perspective and point out if anything untoward is taking place. Part of the manipulator's use of negative reinforcement is the reliance upon the fact that the victim cannot make rational judgments. Friends and other third parties can. By bringing them into the situation the best plans of the manipulator are defeated.

Emotional Frame Control

What It Is

A frame is a way of seeing the world. For example, 'the world is a good and friendly place' is one frame, while 'the world is unfriendly and dangerous' is the opposite frame. Frame control refers to the fact that some people attempt to influence and outright control the way in which others see the world. Emotional frame control refers to a specific focus on controlling how people perceive their emotional makeup at any given time.

A famous concept related to emotional frame control is Stockholm Syndrome. This involves a captive developing feelings of compassion, care and even love to their captor after a prolonged period of time. This is due to the fact that the emotions a person feels are entirely at the mercy of the captor. Regardless of how someone is actually feeling, if the captor tells them with another conviction that they feel a certain way, the victim will come to believe it. This is due to the fact that all of the power in this example situation is held by the captor and not the captive.

So how does emotional frame control matter within the context of covert emotional manipulation? Simply put, covert emotional manipulators will, over time, seek to control their victim's perception of their own emotions.

A classic example of this is the abusive relationship that so commonly exists between male and female romantic partners. The male partner may be controlling, jealous, unpredictable and even violent. The female partner, the victim, may feel genuine feelings of hatred and rage towards the man who is making her life so miserable.

Any time the woman tries to express these feelings, however, she is shut down. Her abuser refuses to validate or acknowledge how she is feeling in any way. Instead, the emotional manipulator responds by insisting the couple are very much in love and everything is fine.

Due to the fact that the female partner in this situation is emotionally and often physically distraught, she lacks any ability to believe herself with a measure of conviction. The manipulator as a result holds all of the power in this situation because they appear to have a rational and logical explanation of what is going on. This leads the abused person to gradually accept what they are being told. They develop a form of emotional color blindness, in which they can no longer see things as they truly are.

How It Occurs

Emotional frame control often occurs initially as a response to a cautious and reluctant attempt by the victim to regain some control over a manipulative situation by expressing how they feel. Many victims are hesitant to do this because they are worried their feelings will be met by anger or even violence. This is rarely the case however. Most skilled manipulators will listen calmly, patiently, and then proceed to explain that the victim is mistaken.

Manipulators will often seem genuinely puzzled and confused by the victim's expression of how they feel. They will calmly assert that the victim must be mistaken, that everything is fine and that there is no possible way anyone rational could have a problem with the way the situation is.

It is no exaggeration to say that emotional frame control is a form of brainwashing. Picture it as follows. Imagine if the manipulator was able to remove five letters from the alphabet. Every time the victim spoke of one of these five letters the manipulator would seem confused and insist there were no such letters.

The above analogy is an accurate description of how emotional frame control works. The manipulator removes the emotional language the victim has to express how they really feel. Rather than argue that the victim is wrong, the manipulator just point blank refuses to accept any form of emotion that they do not feel serves their aims or purposes.

How To Resist

One of the absolute keys to avoiding the dangers of emotional frame control is to have someone other than the manipulator to talk things through with. One of the reasons that emotional frame control works so frequently is due to the fact that the victim has no one to discuss how they are feeling with. Because they are forced to take one of two opinions, their own or that of the manipulator, and the manipulator holds all of the power in the situation, the victim will often disregard their feelings and chalk them up to a mistake in perception or understanding.

If, on the other hand, the victim is able to open up to a third party who validates and acknowledges their feelings then it is harder for them to dismiss what they are feeling. It is no longer a case of the victim comparing their own opinion to that of the manipulator. Instead, it is the opinion of the manipulator opposed by not only the victim's own emotional perception but the agreement and support of all of the victim's confidants.

Another way of resisting emotional frame control is to write feelings down in a journal. This is beneficial because of a victim's emotions exist only in their mind then they are nebulous and susceptible to manipulation. Writing them down in black and white, however, makes the feelings more concrete and tangible. It also allows the victim to look back and remind themselves how they were feeling at any given time without filtering the experience through the distorted lens of the manipulator.

Covert Abuse

What It Is

When abuse is undisguised it can sometimes be easier to perceive, understand and escape from. For example, if an abuser punches someone in the face or calls them an extremely harsh name, then it is fairly clear cut what has taken place. Even in the mind of a broken and manipulated person it is likely that part of them will register that what is happening is classed as abuse and it is not in their best interest.

Covert abuse, on the other hand, is far harder to detect and therefore is more of a hidden danger. If undisguised abuse is a gun being pointed directly at someone then covert abuse is someone being in the scope of an unseen sniper without ever realizing it. Because the threat is hidden the victim is unguarded and vulnerable.

Covert abuse is often disguised as being advice or some other form of constructive feedback.

For example, consider the contrast between these two incidents.

Firstly, a man telling a woman 'You are fat, go to the gym, because you disgust me'. This is a clear cut example of a comment which has the potential to hurt someone and damage their self-esteem. The abuse is not hidden or disguised. Although the victim may well be hurt by such remarks they are likely to understand, on some level that the words were intended to hurt them.

Secondly, imagine if a man says 'My ex girlfriend was beautiful and thin, probably the most attractive girl I have been with. She could fit into almost any sized clothing. I was so lucky to have her'.

Now on the surface the second comment has not been directed at the victim at all. The man is simply remembering someone from his past. However, the covert abuse occurs in the insinuations. It's almost like an optical illusion. The mind of the victim does the work for the abuser and applies the opposite of what is being said to herself.

How It Occurs
Covert abuse often occurs when a manipulator gets the sense that overt abuse would dissuade a victim from continuing their interaction. If a manipulator gets the sense that their victim would shut down or otherwise be unresponsive to more direct forms of abuse then they are likely to take the covert approach instead.

A further reason why manipulators value the power of covert abuse so much is because, when carried out properly, it can leave the victim feeling like their manipulator was trying to help them and had their best interests at heart. For example, if a manipulator frequently points out all of the personality flaws they believe their victim has, they can do so under the guise of trying to help them become a better person. The actual effect is to erode the victim's feeling of self worth and instead replace it with self loathing and doubt. At the same time, the victim begins to see their manipulator as a kind and caring figure who is only trying to help them, despite their many flaws. This combination of self-loathing and dependency is a blank canvas for the manipulator to work with.

Covert abuse will often be used by a manipulator to turn a victim's own doubts, problems and insecurities against them. For example, if a victim had confided in a manipulator that they had always doubted their own intelligence, then the manipulator would covertly and discretely call into question the intelligence of the victim whenever possible. Even if this was done in what seemed to be a 'kind' way on the surface, it would trigger very deep rooted feelings of shame within the victim. This is an example of how a skilled manipulator can effectively make a victim manipulate and hurt themselves, provided the right stimulus is present.

How To Resist

The first step to resisting this subtle form of covert abuse is to ensure that the victim has a clear and accurate understanding of what their own strengths and weaknesses actually are. If a victim knows themselves well then it is not as easy for other people to plant ideas in their mind as to where their deficiencies exist.

A second protective step against covert abuse is for the victim to reflect carefully on the real intention of what the manipulative individual is saying. This can help to identify occasions when the manipulator is acting only in their self-interest, even if they appear to be trying to help the victim. Asking the question 'what is this person trying to get out of the situation?' can force the mind to look at things a different way and uncover any nefarious intentions the other individual may have.

Another effective tool is to shut off mentally whenever the manipulative person starts to try and give 'helpful advice'. One technique that can be useful here is a mantra. A mantra is a short repeated phrase. For example, if a manipulator starts to talk about the physical problems he sees in his victim, under the pretense of helping them become more confident, the victim can repeat over and over in their mind 'I am a human being like everyone else, I have good points and bad points, but I accept and love myself'. Forcing the brain to dwell on and consider a counterpoint to that of the manipulator can prevent any covertly abusive statements from going unchallenged.

Changing the subject and refusing to be drawn into the type of discussions which are likely to feature covert abuse is another powerful option. If the victim is able to change the subject or even point blank refuse it, such as by saying 'I'd rather not talk about this, thanks' then covert abuse is no longer possible. This is due to the fact that the manipulator would seem overtly abusive were they to ignore the victim's wishes. Once the abuse is no longer covert it loses its power to undermine a person's own perception of themselves.

Calculated Intimate Sharing

What It Is

When an interaction between two people progresses in a healthy and normal way it is natural that, over the course of time, they disclose things to one another about their lives and the things they have been through. This creates an atmosphere of sharing and connection that enables the two people to feel as if they are able to talk freely.

Calculated intimate sharing is a distortion of this normal process on the behalf of the manipulator. Calculated intimate sharing differs from regular, healthy disclosure in three ways - the timing, the intention and the type of information shared.

Unlike regular sharing that occurs in the course of a friendship, calculated intimate sharing happens a lot faster. Rather than gradually, over a period of time, often years, revealing personal information about what has happened in life, a manipulator will disclose things about their life within a short period of time. This is intended to ensure that the victim feels closer and more connected to the manipulator than would actually have occurred. This difference in purpose is a key difference between calculated and natural sharing.

The type of information that the manipulator shares is another way in which calculated sharing is differentiated from natural sharing. Most people have a sense of what is and is not too much to share with someone depending upon how close they are. The covert emotional manipulator chooses to disregard such concerns and instead shares whatever they feel will bring the victim closer to them in the shortest time possible.

Unsurprisingly, the type of intimate information revealed during calculated intimate sharing is often entirely false. Manipulators are able to invent details of their lives that never happened and all of the details are likely to involve some kind of emotional event that the manipulator has supposedly suffered through. This can end up with the result that several different people have entirely different understandings of the same individual manipulator. Some people may think he is an orphan, others will believe his parents got divorced. The manipulator puts forward whatever biographical information they feel will gain compliance from their victims.

How It Occurs
Calculated intimate sharing occurs early on in the manipulator's interaction with his victim. It occurs at a time when the manipulator has

decided that it would be beneficial to create an artificial emotional bond between them and the person they are seeking to manipulate.

One way in which calculated emotional sharing is skillfully deployed by the manipulator is by pushing the victim into a position where the victim feels they are the one who has requested the information. For example, the manipulator may change their demeanor from happy and outgoing to sad and withdrawn. The victim is likely to inquire if everything is OK. The manipulator will then use this as a chance to begin the process of calculated sharing. By doing it in this way the victim is unaware that the sharing is nothing but an emotional manipulation tactic. Instead, they feel it is genuine information that they had honestly requested!

The manipulator is likely to reinforce this perception in several ways. After sharing a piece of information about their life which is more than likely either a lie or a distortion, the manipulator will often praise the victim and state how amazing it is they feel able to open up to them so easily. This flatters the victim's ego and further reinforces the false, artificial impression that some kind of amazingly deep connection exists between the two of them.

The manipulator is likely to choose information that they feel will elicit the response they desire from a particular victim. For example, if they know the victim has had a bad experience related to their parents, the manipulator may choose to share some similar type of incident. This is to create a sense of rapport and bond between the manipulator and the victim. Skilled manipulators will be careful to ensure there is enough of a difference between the information they convey and that they know about the victim. This helps to prevent their calculated intimate sharing from appearing to be an obvious deception.

How To Resist

The absolute golden rule when encountering possible calculated intimate sharing is to ask yourself 'what I share this about myself with someone at this stage?' Most people will have a gut feeling reaction as to whether something is suitable to be shared or not. Manipulators will do everything in their power to override this gut feeling through flattery and other forms of manipulation. However, if a person is strong willed enough, they can hold onto their initial gut feeling and use it as a guide to help them navigate a calculated sharing situation.

Another way of fighting back against the weapon of calculated sharing is to keep a detailed record of all of the things the manipulator has attempted to share, and then call them out on it from time to time. For example, if a manipulator tells you about a friend who had a serious illness, bring it up in the future but change a detail, like the type of illness or the name of the friend. The manipulator will often have forgotten the precise details of their lie so will agree with whatever is put to them. This is a clear indication and a true red flag that calculated intimate sharing has occurred.

The key reason for calculated emotional sharing on behalf of the manipulator is to elicit a deep emotional reaction that forms an artificial bond between manipulator and victim. It is therefore advisable for the victim to avoid showing any outward signs of caring too much when hearing what may well be calculated intimate sharing. For example, if the manipulator tells some elaborate story about their childhood, a good response is to acknowledge them and change to a related but far less serious topic. For example, the victim may respond with 'Oh interesting, when I was a kid I loved to play board games'. When the manipulator sees their efforts are not having the desired impact they may stop attempting to force a connection in this manner.

People as Pawns

What It Is

If you've ever played chess you will know that pawns are insignificant players in the scheme of the game. They are numerous and less valuable than other pieces of the board. They can also be moved around frequently and easily.

Emotional manipulators are adept at using other people as pawns in their sick mind games. Rather than seeing others as human beings worthy of respect and dignity, a true covert emotional manipulator will only see a chance to influence their victim in one way or another.

This can be carried out in a few different ways. Sometimes, the emotional manipulator will use a third party in an attempt to create jealousy. For example, in the context of a romantic relationship, the manipulator may praise the physical qualities of a woman who is not the one he is with. This is often done in a way which emphasizes the other woman having traits that the woman he is with knows she does not have herself. For example, if the manipulator's girlfriend is short, he may praise how beautiful taller girls are.

It is important to note that the people that the manipulator talks about and attempts to use for such purposes often fail to actually exist. Some manipulators will go to extreme lengths in order to create fictional pawns in their emotional games. It is not uncommon for manipulators to create elaborate online profiles of other people and then use these profiles to message either the victim or their own, real profile.

Manipulators can also use other people as adversaries of their victim. For example, the manipulator may manufacture some form of struggle or bad feeling between the two individuals. This gives the manipulator the chance to step in and play the good guy, the knight in shining armor. The victim will often feel so happy to feel as if someone is on their side they won't stop and question how the situation could have arisen in the first place.

How It Occurs

Introducing a third party, or third parties, into a manipulation often occurs because the manipulator is worried that their own efforts at manipulation are losing some of their power. Some people gradually lose their ability to be influenced by a specific person over time. If the manipulator senses this is happening then they may decide that a third party is needed in order to regain the balance of power in the interaction.

One tactic that is often used by manipulators with regards to their third party approach is to seed the idea of the third party long before they actually have a prominent role in the manipulation. If, for example, the manipulator has often mentioned a person they know by name, regardless of whether this person actually exists or not, it will seem less strange when the person suddenly crops up in the future. Skilled manipulators are careful to build up to the introduction of a third party carefully so it does not come as a surprise or shock to their victim.

The personal traits of the third party will often be carefully chosen to elicit a particular response in the victim. For example, if the victim has a problem with a certain type of person, such as extroverts or popular people, it is likely the manipulator will draw upon this knowledge and present the third party as being something that they know will hurt the victim.

Real people known to either the manipulator, victim or both are another way in which the manipulator can seek to use others in their pursuit of control over a victim. Real people have the advantage for the manipulator of being more believable than some fictional creation of their own mind. Real people, on the other hand, have the disadvantage of being harder to control. They may say or do something which is not conducive to the manipulative effect the manipulator wishes them to have. This means that often any real person involved will be geographically distant from the victim and manipulator. This allows the manipulator to project any qualities onto the person they wish as they will never be around in person to give a different impression.

How To Resist

It is, of course, possible that genuine situations with third parties will arise that have nothing to do with a manipulator. It is easy to determine whether a third party involvement is genuine or the product of manipulation. If the third party is real then it should be relatively easy for the victim to reach out and contact the person. In the case of online only profiles there should be pictures of the third party with other people. Simply contact the other people and check out the story that has been put forward. Often, there will either be major discrepancies between the events as the manipulator has explained, and the reality of the situation, and sometimes the victim will be unable to find a single person who actually knows the invented third person!

Another way of dealing with the introduction of a third party is to fight fire with fire, so to speak. If the manipulator brings up a third party, bring up one of your own! Don't do it in a manipulative or calculated way, and definitely don't create fictional characters, but be sure to let the manipulator know you are not passively sitting through whatever they wish to do. If they can do something, you can do it too. Many manipulators will hate this leveling of the playing field and may even move on to another victim entirely as a result.

Considering whether a newly mentioned third party conveniently serves the purpose of the manipulator is another valuable tool to use in your fight back. If, for example, it would suit the manipulator for you to be jealous, and suddenly a third party is mentioned who you naturally are expected to be jealous of, this is a major red flag that games are being played at your expense.

Reacting very nonchalantly to anything can be a good way to reduce the power of this tactic. For example, should your romantic partner mention an ex of theirs who has some physical trait you do not, just reply with the minimum level of politeness, conveying disinterest. 'Oh, really? Fair enough'. If the manipulator sees the third party is not having the desired impact on you, don't be surprised if they magically disappear and are not mentioned again!

It's All Your Fault

What It Is

One of the absolute classic moves on the behalf of an emotional manipulator is finding a way to make the victim feel responsible for anything bad that has happened. This can be something bad that the manipulator has done or said or something from an entirely different period of their life! Let's illustrate this idea with some examples.

Emotional manipulators in romantic relationships are infamous for their ability to get the victim to blame and doubt their own self. For example, if a manipulator is physically violent towards their victim, they will find a way to blame the victim. Some examples include saying things like 'Well you made me angry', 'I was acting in self defense' or 'It was an accident, I was trying to just hold you still'. This may sound farfetched but in the weakened emotional state of the victim such reasons, if put forward with enough conviction and certainty by the manipulator, can begin to sound convincing.

A more discrete, but equally devastating, form of victim blaming is delving into the victim's past and making them feel responsible for the bad parts. For example, if the victim has told the manipulator their parents divorced when they were young, the manipulator may, in the future, say something like 'I can't believe how much stress your parents were under after you were born, I could never have dealt with that, no one could. It's good they broke up and are happier now'.

The effect of blaming the victim is twofold. Firstly, it creates a cognitive pattern in the victim's mind that everything bad is their fault. This makes further manipulation and abuse seem more acceptable in the victim's mind. Secondly, the manipulator is likely to use examples they know the victim secretly feels to be true. If a victim believes they do in fact have a part to play in their parents' divorce then a manipulator implying this doesn't feel like manipulation. It just feels like the truth that the victim had feared all along.

How It Occurs
The primary reason that the manipulator is able to get away with blaming the victim for the negative things that occur is because the victim

lacks any power in the situation. The imbalance that exists between the two parties means that the manipulator almost has a position of control and authority over the victim. In practical terms this means that if the manipulator says something is one way, it is often easier and less demanding of the victim to simply agree, than to rationally figure out how it is not the case.

Like many other of the manipulative tactics we have explored, victim blaming often begins gradually and about small things. For example, if a victim is late for something, or misses something, the manipulator will be sure to discretely point out how this is the responsibility of the victim. This begins to create a perception in the mind of the victim of their incompetence and bad judgment. Such a perception can be exploited with regards to more serious things by the manipulator further down the line.

The most diabolical manipulators will occasionally find something that genuinely is the victim's fault and present this alongside various things which certainly aren't. This has the impact of taking away the victim's ability to say 'everything I get blamed for is not actually my fault' as there will be a few examples to contradict this. If the victim sees that the manipulator is right from time to time then they will be more willing to accept they are right all of the time.

Rather than finding cunning ways of placing blame on the victim, manipulators will often take a 'moral high ground' stance which leads to the victim to blame themselves without the manipulator directly doing so! For example, if something bad or unlucky has happened to the victim, the manipulator may strongly imply that people should take personal responsibility and own their mistakes. Although the manipulator has not talked directly about the victim, they have subconsciously led the victim towards reaching the conclusion that they are in fact in the wrong.

How To Resist

Victim blaming is only effective if the victim places importance upon who or what is to blame for events. A powerful way to resist the effects of victim blaming is by clearly and repeatedly stating and, more importantly, showing that attributing blame is of low importance to the victim.

For example, if the victim is blamed for something, such as missing out on an opportunity, rather than showing that they are deeply reflective about this and feel guilty, the victim is better served by saying 'Oh well, what's done is done, just have to move on now". This takes away the power that the manipulator has. If the victim is able to demonstrate they don't care about why things have happened, even if they secretly do, it takes away from the power of the manipulator to hold blame over the head of the victim.

Hinting

What It Is

One of the most powerful weapons in the arsenal of a manipulator is the ability to hint at a negative outcome without saying it outright. The power of suggestion is incredibly strong and, when deployed well, a hint can cause more distress and pain to the mind of a victim than a clear cut statement. This is due to the fact that hinting leaves room for ambiguity and allows the victim to create their own ideas and worries about what may befall them.

Some of the most common ways that a manipulator will use hints against their victim include mixing in an ominous hint amidst seemingly normal conversation. For example, the manipulator may be discussing something fairly mundane, like a news story, and then turn to the victim, making strong eye contact, and hint that something as bad as the news story they were discussing may happen to the victim if they are not careful.

It is useful to think of the hint as a seed which the manipulator plants in the mind of the victim. One small comment, remark, facial expression or gesture is all it takes for the seed to take root. Then, amidst a climate of fear, worry and stress, the victim is left to ruminate on the hint and what was intended by it. Often, the victim's own mind is capable of producing far worse scenarios than anything the manipulator would actually carry out.

The hint is particularly distressing as it cannot be mentioned to the manipulator as nothing clear cut has been said. This allows for the manipulator to have a clear stance of deniability should the victim attempt to call them out on their hinting. This can leave the victim paranoid and scared as to whether they have actually been threatened or whether they have imagined it. The insecurity created by this doubt leaves the victim susceptible to further manipulation.

How It Occurs

The manipulator will typically use the hint when they feel that out and out threats or lies are losing their power to make their victim feel terrified and controlled. If the manipulator senses that their victim is prone to over thinking or has some type of paranoid tendencies then they are likely to see the hint as an effective tool that they can use against them.

Like many other tactics that manipulators use, hints are likely to be tested out initially before being deployed on a frequent basis. This will usually involve the manipulator hinting that something bad may take place and then judging the reaction of the victim. For example, the victim and the manipulator may be talking about going on vacation. The manipulator may say something along the lines of 'I've heard some people are killed while abroad and it is made to look like an accident' in an intonation which is intended to clearly link this outcome to the victim. If the manipulator notices that the victim appears worried, scared or thoughtful then it increases the likelihood that the hint will be used again in the future. If the victim seems not to pick up on the hint or it does not bother them much then the manipulator is more likely to use a different tactic in the future.

Advanced level manipulators often deploy a succession of hints over time that are intended to layer the levels of fear and mistrust that are present in the mind of their victims. By the end of this process many manipulators are able to induce a feeling of sheer panic and terror in their victim with only a few words that to anyone on the outside would seem absolutely innocuous and nothing to worry about. This is a clear sign that hints are a dangerous weapon in the hands of a true manipulator and their danger grows the longer they are allowed to continue for.

How To Resist
The main way that victims can fight back against the power of hints is by ensuring that if

something negative is hinted at they do not overly react. This response is likely to increase the likelihood that the manipulator tries some other type of tactic instead. It can be difficult at first to not show concern at hints as they can be very ominous and threatening.

One of the key ways to ensure that a victim is able to react calmly to hints is by understanding on a deep level that if a manipulator is going to carry out some kind of negative action then they will do it regardless of if the victim worries about it or not. Because of this it is beneficial to the victim to avoid worrying as it will not change anything or help them in any way. In fact, the less a victim is able to worry, the stronger they will be mentally. Mental strength allows the victim to retain greater control over their own emotions and thus be less susceptible to further attempts at emotional control.

Another way of resisting the destructive power of manipulative hints is to carefully reflect upon the

types of discussions and situations that usually
lead to hints being used by the manipulator. If,
for example, talking about the future is
something which usually prompts a threatening
hint, then steering the conversation away from
this topic is particularly beneficial. By
understanding the common aspects of the
manipulator's hints the victim is able to ensure
they avoid the pitfalls which may lead to them
being used.

Empty Words

What It Is

Unlike many of the other tactics used by
manipulators, empty words may seem innocuous
and even kind to someone who is unaware of
their purpose. Empty words can be understood
as things said by the manipulator which they do
not feel or consider to be true on a deep level.
They will often adapt their empty words to the
specific psychological nuances of their victim.

Some examples of the most common types of empty words used include declarations of love which the manipulator does not feel, promises of commitment which the manipulator does not intend to keep and compliments which are insincere and designed to pander to the insecurities of the person who is being manipulated.

There is no set formula for the type of empty words that will be spoken or the purpose behind them. Different types of manipulators will use empty words in different ways. Generally though, the words will be intended to get a reaction from the victim without the manipulator having to actually put in any effort. For example, if the manipulator wants the victim to feel feelings of love towards them, then using empty words can achieve this effect without the manipulator actually having to feel or display love or anything resembling it on a genuine level.

Empty words can also be used in a negative way. For example, the manipulator may threaten to self-harm or even commit suicide without any real intention of following up on the words. Some manipulators even have carefully calculated routines involving the deployment of alternating positive and negative sentiments. These are intended to confuse and overwhelm the victim's emotional response centers of the brain.

How It Occurs

Empty words are usually deployed throughout the course of a manipulation. They often begin in the earliest stages of an interaction between the victim and their manipulator and continue until the manipulation eventually ends for whatever reason.

In the earliest stage of the relationship between the victim and the manipulator empty words may be used to create a sense of dependency. By declaring strong feelings for the victim which don't actually exist the manipulator is able to ensure that the victim develops an attachment and reliance on them which is based on fantasy rather than actuality.

For someone who has not experienced the effects of manipulative empty words it may seem unlikely that they would work. The key to their use however is not in the words that are said but in the tone and other forms of sub communication of the person speaking them. For example, experienced manipulators are likely to be able to deliver such empty words in a tone of voice and with a facial expression and body language that convinces the victim of their sincerity.

The manipulator also relies on the fact that the victim will often find it easier to accept what is being told to them than to question everything the manipulator has ever said. If, for example, the victim decides that the manipulator is lying then it requires them to reexamine everything they feel to be true about the manipulator. Human beings prefer to confirm what they believe rather than challenging it. Due to this, many victims will simply accept the empty words that are spoken to them because doing so is easier than doubting everything they have ever known.

How To Resist

The golden rule when it comes to resisting the power of empty words is to cross reference the words with the actual actions of the manipulative person. For example, one of the most commonly used empty word phrases by manipulators are declarations of love and affection. If someone hears such things being spoken but questions how true they are it is worth examining the behavior of the person who has spoken them. Do they act affectionately or do they merely claim to? Often, by cross referencing words and behavior, victims will be able to expose the inconsistencies and flaws in what their manipulator is telling them.

It is also worth holding onto memories of when the manipulator has proved to be inconsistent or false in the past. If the victim is able to hold onto the idea in their mind that the manipulator is a person who cannot be trusted, or cannot be fully trusted, then it makes it easier to shatter the false picture that the manipulator seeks so desperately to portray.

Seeming to agree with the manipulator while internally doubting and questioning them is another valuable and powerful way to resist a manipulator's clutches. It is often problematic to out and out contradict a manipulator as it can incur anger and even physical violence. Pacifying the manipulator by accepting what they say is the best method as long as internally the person holds onto the belief that the manipulator cannot be trusted and is someone who lies and distorts the truth.

Denying Reality

What It Is

One of the scariest and most disturbing things a person can experience is questioning their own sanity. A fundamental thing that all human beings rely on is being able to trust their own perception of the world and the information that their five senses present to them. When the trust in one's own sanity goes it can be the hardest thing to deal with. People are used to dealing with fear and even violence but insanity is something no one ever expects to deal with. For this reason it can be the most powerful weapon in a manipulator's toolkit to make someone question their own sanity.

One of the main ways that a person can be made to feel insane is by denying what they perceive to be real. This can take various forms. The basic theory behind denying someone's reality is that when the manipulator holds the balance of power in a relationship they are able to dictate to their victim what is and is not real.

Think of a parent and a child. Because the parent is far more powerful than the child, and the child is reliant upon the parent, the child is accepting of whatever the parent tells them. This is comparable to manipulators and victims. Because the manipulator holds the power in the situation and has induced reliance upon them on behalf of the victim then the victim accepts what they are told.

Denying reality is rarely as simple or straightforward as the manipulator telling the victim 'that's not true, you are wrong'. Instead, the manipulator is able to suggest, imply and infer a different version of reality than the one perceived by the victim. What makes this tactic especially devastating is the ability of the manipulator to act as if they are being kind and patient while setting the victim straight. This can leave the victim feeling very confused as to both the truth of a situation and also the manipulator's motives and intentions.

How It Occurs

The manipulator is likely to begin testing a victim's susceptibility to being manipulated in this way relatively early on. For example, a common way to begin this tactic is for the manipulator to begin contradicting small details about what has happened. The victim may bring up a memory such as a meal that the two ate together. The manipulator will change some small detail, such as what they ordered, even though they know that the victim's version of events is in fact correct. This sets a pattern and establishes in the victim's mind that their own memory is questionable and cannot be fully relied upon.

Over time, the manipulator is likely to increase the frequency and severity of the type of things they deny the reality of. It is likely that what begins as an occasional tactic will become more commonplace. What starts as minor details, such as the example of the details of a shared meal, will become more and more significant. The manipulator may even be able to convince the victim that they have remembered details of their own lives incorrectly.

If the victim ever calls out the manipulator on what is happening the manipulator is able to say something along the lines of 'well, you know you are forgetful, remember when this happened?' By drawing on the early, seemingly insignificant moments of reality denial, the manipulator is able to use them as a weapon and form of evidence when it comes to more serious and significant denials.

How To Resist

One of the best ways to resist reality denial is by keeping a secret journal. This can be a paper journal or, if this is likely to be discovered, a hidden file on a smartphone or computer. If the victim is beginning to question their own sense of reality about a certain topic then they can refer back to their journal and check what actually happened. The reason that the manipulator is able to make a victim question reality is due to the fact that the manipulator's word goes against the victim's, and the manipulator holds the psychological balance of power. By introducing a third party, such as a diary, the victim is able to refer back to someone other than the manipulator.

Another form of useful third party that can help to combat a manipulator's denial of reality is a trusted friend or relative. If the victim shares details of their life with the manipulator with someone else, then they can check with this person as to what they told them. This is similar to the diary or journal insofar as it allows the victim to gain a perspective on events that is outside of the immediate situation.

Minimizing

What It Is

Minimizing occurs when the manipulator tries to downplay the significance of something that has occurred. This can be either an event that has taken place or a feeling that the victim wishes to express. This is done in order to leave the victim feeling as if their feelings are not significant. It also serves the dual purpose of undermining the victim's trust in their own judgment and feelings.

There are a lot of different psychological reasons behind minimizing. Firstly, it allows the manipulator to become an emotional dictator of the situation. By being able to state how serious something is, or is not, it gives the manipulator further power and control over most situations.

Some manipulators also use minimizing as a way of protecting their own interests. For example, if a victim threatens to tell someone what has been taking place, such as in the case of an emotionally abusive relationship, then the manipulator may seek to downgrade the likelihood of this occurring by minimizing. If they can convince the victim that what has happened is not serious then it can lead to a reduction in the chance of the manipulator getting caught out or exposed for the abusive, manipulative behavior they have been carrying out.

Minimizing also serves the purpose of inducing a feeling of guilt and shame in the victim. If the victim feels that they have reacted strongly or inappropriately to something that has happened then they may feel bad and as if their reaction was inappropriate in some way. This can lead to the victim feeling as if they are in the wrong rather than the manipulator being at fault. Once in this position of guilt and regret they become vulnerable to further manipulative and self-esteem eroding tactics being used against them.

How It Occurs

There are many different situations that minimizing may be used by a manipulator. Some of the most common will now be explored along with an explanation of why they occur and what the manipulator is attempting to achieve by using minimization in these contexts.

Physical abuse is one scenario where minimization can occur. For example, if the manipulator had become violent and hit their victim, and the victim complained about this, the manipulator may deny any hitting had taken place. Instead they may say something like they tried to hold the victim to calm them down or that the victim had inflicted the injury upon their own self. Often minimization is used in this situation in order to simultaneously protect the manipulator from possible repercussions in the form of police attention while also undermining the victim's trust in their own memory.

Emotional abuse is another situation which is ripe for manipulation at the hands of a manipulator. For example, if a victim feels that they are emotionally distraught following a heated argument, the manipulator may seek to downplay either the intensity of the argument, the victim's emotional response or both. This seeks to remove blame from the manipulator for what has happened and, like all other forms of minimization, also reduces the victim's trust in their own recollection of events and how they feel about them.

How To Resist

Resisting minimization can be something that is very difficult to effectively achieve. For a regular person it may seem easy to have an accurate understanding of events that have taken place. For example, anyone would assume that they would have a clear understanding as to whether they have been physically abused and the events which led up to the violence. However, the victims of manipulators are not in a position to see things clearly. They are broken down by constant tactics such as those you are now learning about. Because of this, their minds are susceptible to influence and misdirection.

There are, however, things a victim can do to resist minimization and its impact. One valuable tool is to write down what has taken place soon after it has happened. The memory is fragile and prone to forgetfulness. Because of this mental fallibility a victim will often feel unsure that their understanding of something that has happened is actually true. If, however, they are able to produce a written record of events soon after they have taken place then this can lead to reassurance.

It is often a good idea to not argue when the manipulator tries to minimize something. Arguing can lead to the manipulator becoming angry and deploying further hatred and violence. Instead, the victim should passively accept what the manipulator is saying while, in their own mind, holding firm to the true version of events. This allows the victim to both understand that an event was in fact serious, not minimal, while protecting against further abuse from the manipulator.

Withdrawing
What It Is

Withdrawing is known by several different names, all of which indicate the same basic manipulative tactic. The other terms are freezing out, putting up a wall and blanking. This refers to the practice of the manipulator refusing to engage with their victim. This may involve a physical withdrawal, e.g moving to a different room from them, a refusal to listen to them or a refusal to speak or engage in responses. These are not mutually exclusive and several types of withdrawal may occur at the same time.

Withdrawal can range in severity from a total ignoring of the victim to a partial acknowledgement mixed in with mostly ignoring. This latter tactic is particularly impactful as the victim is unable to say they are being ignored totally. Rather, the manipulator increases the frustration that the victim feels by paying them just enough attention while mostly freezing them out.

Withdrawal can happen either in person or via distance. An example of withdrawal occurring through distance would be a manipulator who chooses to not reply to any messages or phone calls from the victim. Some manipulators will completely switch up in person and act like nothing ever happened. This leaves the victim insecure, chasing and totally unsure of where they stand. All of these aspects lessen the power of the victim and put the power in the hands of the manipulator.

How It Occurs

A common time for withdrawal to be used is when the manipulator has provoked the victim into a state of anger or annoyance. For example, the manipulator may instigate an argument or begin to insult the victim in order to anger them and get their emotions going. Once the victim has reached the point of exasperation and rage the manipulator turns ice cold and refuses to participate in the argument any further. This is incredibly frustrating for the victim as it means the manipulator has complete control over the situation.

There is no set situation which will trigger the withdrawal. However, it is often used if the manipulator wishes to reinforce the sense of control they have over a situation. By provoking the victim into feeling a strong emotion and then withdrawing completely, the manipulator is dictating the emotional tempo of the interaction. This reinforces on both a literal and subconscious level that the manipulator is the one in control.

The manipulator is likely to find out the type of withdrawal technique that gets under the victim's skin the most and use that. For example, if the manipulator tries shutting down verbally one time, and the victim is provoked into a mixture of rage and despair, then this increases the likelihood that the manipulator will repeat this technique in the future.

How To Resist

Withdrawal only works if the victim is willing to chase after the manipulator's emotional lead and try and force a response when one is not forthcoming. The best way to deal with a withdrawal tactic is to not play into the manipulator's hands and instead just choose to ignore what is taking place. If the manipulator tries to freeze out the victim, and the victim doesn't rise to the bait, then the technique loses all of its power.

A similar principle applies over text message and other distance methods of communication. If the manipulator provokes the victim into seeking a response, such as by issuing a threat or strong emotional statement over text message, and then refuses to respond, the victim should immediately stop chasing. By refusing to chase after the manipulator the victim is depriving them of the reaction that they are seeking. By showing they are not so easily led by the manipulator's actions, the manipulator is less likely to try this technique in the future.

Lying

What It Is

Almost everyone lies in one way or the other. Just because a lie is told it does not mean that the person telling it is automatically a covert emotional manipulator. Instead, it's not the lying which indicates someone is a manipulator, but the way in which they lie. The frequency, severity and purpose of the lying are all factors which help to determine whether lies are being told from a manipulative perspective or not.

Lying has a range of different purposes. Some manipulators lie in order to cover up where they have been. For example, in the case of an emotional manipulator who is romantically involved with their victim but are cheating on them, lies may be told in order to cover up their actual activities and locations. Lying can also be used to gain sympathy for the manipulator. For example, one of the most common types of lies that are told are elaborate sob stories about the background of the manipulator. They may tell untrue tales of an arduous childhood including abuse and neglect.

One of the key features of manipulative lying is that it is often told in a way which makes it difficult to disprove. For example, the manipulator will avoid including any concrete facts which could be either verified or dismissed by the victim. Instead, the manipulator will focus on vague and imprecise statements. This gives the victim no way of conclusively checking out whether a story is or is not true.

Different manipulators vary in the amount they lie. For some people, it is all they know. Almost everything that some manipulators say will be untrue. Other manipulators use lies more sparingly. For example, some manipulators will carefully blend stories which contain grains of truth and a heavy helping of lies also. This means that if a detail in the story is true, such as a location or time period, and the victim checks this, it lends credence to the untrue aspects and suggests they are true as well.

How It Occurs

Lying will often be used in the initial stage of a manipulation. Some manipulators lie about every last detail including their name, age, background and employment status. In the case of the bigamist and fraud categories of manipulators, basically nothing they say at all will be true. The initial stage of lying is often to establish an identity which is far from the truth. This is a foundation upon which the rest of the manipulation will continue.

Although the early stages of the manipulation are a common time for lying to occur, they are by no means the only time. If a manipulator sees an impact upon the victim as a result of their lying then they are likely to keep it up. After all, there is no use in letting go of a technique which is serving their aims.

Some manipulators are adept at weaving a complex web of lies with no contradictions or other inconsistencies. Others, less so. Sometimes the victim will pick up on some factual error or improbability within a story. Calling out the manipulator on such lies, however, is unlikely to lead to a good outcome. This is due to the fact that the manipulator will usually manage to either swerve the attention away from the topic that the victim has mentioned or find some other way to avoid telling the truth. They may try a range of tactics including telling the victim they have remembered or understood incorrectly, insisting that the topic is too painful to talk about or out and out ignoring the victim's requests to discuss the matter.

How To Resist

One of the prerequisites for resisting lying is having a preexisting level of common sense and an ear for the truth. If a victim is a generally naive and gullible person then it is easier for a manipulator to lie to them without consequence. If, however, the victim is otherwise able to detect when a story doesn't ring true then they stand a better chance of resisting the lies of a manipulator.

Keeping track of what the manipulator has told the victim is another way of exposing a manipulator as a liar. Most manipulators rely on the fallibility of the human memory to avoid being detected in their untruth. If the victim is able to write down what they have been told, such as in a smartphone or journal, then they have a way of fact checking the stories that are being fed to them and finding any contradictions and inconsistencies.

Telling a manipulator that you know they are lying is a risky game to play and is generally best avoided. This is due to the fact that manipulators will basically never admit to being caught out in a lie. The only time they will admit to a lie is if they will receive some type of benefit from it.

The best option when catching a manipulative person lying is simply to register the fact they are lying, make a mental note that the person is not trustworthy and do not call them out on it. Anything other than this approach is likely to cause even more of a problem and not lead to anything constructive whatsoever.

Omission

What It Is

Omission is similar to lying insofar as it involves a distortion of the truth. However, in the case of lying, the manipulator actively provides untrue information. In the case of omission, the manipulator avoids stating true information in order to present a misleading picture of reality. There are many different situations in which omission may be the tactic that a manipulator feels will work the best, however, the underlying purpose for omission is always roughly the same.

Basically put, omission is used in order to allow the victim to understand things a certain way, when in actual fact, they are another way entirely.

Omission is a favored tactic of manipulators as it provides them with deniability. Unlike lying, omission does not involve actively saying anything false, rather just avoiding saying things that the manipulator does not feel will serve their interests. Due to this, if the victim chooses to raise the subject of omission with the manipulator, the recourse is always available that 'I didn't ever tell you anything different'.

The other reason why omission is so widely used is due to the fact that it can be turned around on the victim if the manipulator so desires. For example, if the victim calls the manipulator out on some piece of information they have failed to mention, then the manipulator can guilt trip them into feeling as if they are being invasive, not respecting privacy and asking inappropriate questions.

How It Occurs

The type of information that the manipulator chooses to omit depends entirely upon the way in which they are hoping to manipulate their victim. Some of the most common situations featuring omission will now be explored and the way in which omission is used in each explained.

In the case of romantic manipulation, the manipulator will often omit if they have other partners, spouses or children. This is to present a picture of themselves if as available and something desirable to their victim. If the victim were to know the manipulator was involved with other women or men then the victim would never open their heart and mind to the manipulator. This would prevent the manipulation from beginning and entirely thwart the manipulator's plans.

Financial manipulators will often hide their true circumstances from the one they are trying to extract money from. For example, many experienced manipulators will have a practiced sob story of how hard their life is and how they have so many expenses that they are unable to meet. They may neglect to tell the victim that they have a lot of money saved up or some other detail which would shatter the picture they are trying to paint.

The general guiding principle when considering whether omission is taking place is that, if the information were brought to the victim's attention, it would lessen the emotional grip that the manipulator had established on the victim's psyche. Therefore whatever is not being said is something that would contradict the carefully crafted lie the manipulator has invested time and effort into establishing.

How To Resist

Resisting omission is difficult. One of the most common and obvious ways to try and protect against it is by asking questions regarding information the victim feels that the manipulator is withholding. For example, direct questions such as 'are you married?' or 'have you ever been in jail?'. This may seem to make sense, however it is unlikely to work. This is due to the fact that the type of emotional manipulator who has no qualms in omitting key facts about their life will often have no problem with lying to cover up such omissions.

One of the best ways to fight back against the tactic of omission is by doing some independent research into what you feel the manipulator may be hiding. For example, take a look at their social media profiles and see if there are any red flags. Although it seems underhanded, if you know the person you are dealing with is a manipulator, do not be scared to check through their phone when they are not around. Be very careful with this however as if caught, the manipulator may fly into a severe rage, even turning violent. Always err on the side of caution and self protection when trying to find out the truth about what a manipulator has perhaps "forgot" to mention.

Never Owning Up

What It Is

Have you ever come across a badly behaved child who will never admit to something they have done wrong? Or an overly entitled teenager who will always have a finger ready to point at what or whoever is to blame for their latest misfortune? Some emotional manipulators are the master of never owning up to what they have done. The emotional manipulator's use of this tactic is chilling and dangerous however. Understanding how it happens and why is a key element in retaining a semblance of mental control on behalf of the victim.

Basically, no matter what a manipulator has done, it absolutely is not their fault at all. Some manipulator's genuinely believe this due to the fact they are narcissistic sociopaths without a conscience. Other manipulators are fully aware that they are to blame for things, and that they have done wrong, but they choose to lie and conceal this fact in order to serve their own manipulative intentions.

Some manipulators will actively deny being responsible for things with the use of phrases such as "that wasn't my fault" or "I didn't do that". Others are more subtle in their shirking of responsibility. If they are blamed for something they will just look puzzled or even upset. The best manipulators will remain calm and never become heated or intense over any accusations that are leveled towards them. This calmness can unsettle the victim into actually doubting whether the manipulator is in fact responsible for anything at all!

How It Occurs
Being blamed for physical occurrences is one situation that many manipulators will commonly

refuse to take any blame for whatsoever. For example, if a manipulator grabbed their victim in the course of an argument, and this left some bruising on them, the manipulator will insist that the bruising must have happened some other way. They will not get defensive or aggressive when carrying out their denial. Instead, they will simply look puzzled and even amused as if the victim has gone utterly mad. This is often intended to make the victim lose their temper and further reinforce the perception of the manipulator as the calm person and the victim as the unhinged individual, even though the opposite is always true.

Denying the consequences of their actions or words is another area in which manipulators are especially adept. For example, if a manipulative person loses their job, they will never attribute this to their own actions. Instead, something outside of their control will take the blame! This is often tied up into a grand conspiracy in which the manipulator portrays that they are a persecuted person who is only trying to do good in the world. If this portrayal is challenged or doubted then the manipulator will almost always have a long list of reasons and examples why it is true. Trying to argue against it is tiring and futile.

Interestingly, some manipulators will increase the mind games aspect of their denial of responsibility by attempting to take the blame for things which are not their fault. This will usually provoke the victim into reassuring the manipulator that they are not in fact responsible for those particular events. This allows the manipulator to claim they are someone who is more than willing to take responsibility for things. They will never point out that they only take responsibility for the wrong things however, and even that is just another layer of manipulation!

How To Resist

The key to not succumbing to a denial of responsibility is not seeking accountability from a manipulator in the first place. If the victim is able to fix in their mind the fact that they are dealing with a manipulative person who will say or do anything without hesitation, should it serve them, then the victim can focus on finding a workable exit strategy from the situation rather than seeking normal, moral behavior from the manipulator.

As mentioned above, many manipulators will falsely take responsibility for things they have not done purely to elicit a reassurance from the person they are manipulating! Avoid falling into this trap. If you notice a manipulative person is trying to take the blame for something they have not done, then resist the urge to set the matter straight. Instead, simply say something along the lines of "It's OK" or "Don't worry about it". This is one of the few times you might be able to expose some cracks in the expertly manipulative facade. Some manipulators will give the game away by insisting on apologizing further. No matter what they say or do, refuse to reassure them. Just be as calm and blank as possible. Anything else is simply providing further material for the manipulator to work with.

Gaslighting

What It Is

Of all the tactics in this book, gaslighting is perhaps the most chilling, devious and out and out evil of them all. Why? Because gaslighting is nothing less than the deliberate, persistent and intended process of making another human being become insane.

Where does the term gaslighting come from? There is an old theatre production which is a textbook study in the process of emotional manipulation. It features a psychopathic, abusive husband who slowly drives his wife insane by making her question her own memory and judgment. The name 'gaslighting' comes from one technique used by the husband which was to alter the brightness of some lights gradually over time and then, when the wife questioned this, insist there was no change at all.

Manipulators will often begin the process of gaslighting by removing anything that may be considered an anchor of sanity for the victim. So, if the victim has a best friend that helps to keep them grounded and give them good advice, the manipulator will do everything in their power to stop this friend from being around. The same goes for members of the victim's family, their religious beliefs and anything else which can help them make sense of the world around them.

The manipulator will then start to make gradual but noticeable changes which impact upon the victim, a prime example being the changing of the lights in which this tactic gets its name from. The manipulator will usually start by changing one small thing but over time will begin to change multiple things at once. This adds a layered aspect where the victim will begin to question their own sanity. If the technique goes on for long enough then the victim will even start to see changes where there are none. This is advanced level manipulation which will often result in the victim needing extensive psychological therapy should they ever escape the situation.

How It Occurs

A few of the most common situations where gaslighting is used will now be explored.

Physical gaslighting is often the first step in the manipulator's deployment of this tactic. They will start to make small physical changes to the environment of the victim. For example, the manipulator may change the toothpaste that the victim uses or move the contents of one cupboard to another and vice versa. Put yourself in the victim's shoes. What is more likely, that their toothpaste has been nefariously swapped, or they have simply forgotten? By getting the victim to accept this one small change as being a product of their own bad memory then the process of gaslighting has begun.

As well as physical gaslighting, factual gaslighting is another common usage of this devious technique. This involves the manipulator making the victim question their perception of facts over time. For example, the manipulator may insist that some small facts the victim has remembered are wrong. This may be the names of places they have been to or details about their daily routine.

Once a victim has lost trust of their own mind, a manipulator may be able to make absolutely drastic levels of manipulation occur. For example, there are cases on the record of victims who have forgotten their own true names or dates of birth as a result of their sanity being mercilessly exploited like a toy.

The manipulator will often deprive the victim of things that help to keep them sane. For example, the manipulator may deprive the victim of sleep, insist they drink alcohol and restrict their access to the outside world. Anything that could be used as some kind of cultish mind control technique is likely to feature in the gaslighter's repertoire.

How To Resist

Resisting gaslighting is of absolute drastic importance. This is due to the fact that the price for failing to do so is no less than the victim's own sanity. Even physical abuse can be recovered from but gaslighting can lead to people spending the rest of their life in psychiatric wards. Google the topic if you don't believe this. Let it again be stated. Resist gaslighting or risk losing your mind, forever.

So how to stop this manifestation of pure, calculated evil? The first step is to do everything in your power to anchor yourself to reality and your own sanity. If a manipulator is trying to stop you from contacting someone, be sure to keep contacting them. They are likely a grounded person who will help to keep you grounded and sane. Make sure you get plenty of sleep, do not drink excessively and try and keep a diary of what is happening in your life. All of these should be temporary measures as finding a way out should be your ultimate goal. The type of person who will gaslight is the type of person who will stop at nothing in their pursuit of your ruin.

The key mental approach to resisting gaslighting can be summarized in one word - acceptance. Do not question or fight back against changes you are noticing. An object has moved? Fine, ignore it. Your manipulator is contradicting a fact you know to be true? Fine, let them. Resistance and mental turmoil is the product of gaslighting. If you do not allow the changes to get to you then you will not begin the process of losing your sanity. Rather than expending your energy on calling out your manipulator, begin secretly plotting your escape. The exit strategies chapter of this book will help you with this. Act with haste as even the strongest person can succumb to the mind games of a skilled manipulator eventually.

Diversion and Evasion

What It Is

Pinning down a manipulator and getting a straight answer from them can be as difficult as herding cats. Anyone who has experience of dealing with a manipulative individual will be well aware that they have a seemingly unlimited amount of ways to avoid being truthful or responding to something that they do not wish to.

Diversion and evasion are closely related but slightly different. Diversion involves the manipulator changing the focus of a conversation to something other than what the victim wishes it to be. Think of a road closure. The victim wants to go one way but the manipulator sends them down a different road entirely. Evasion is simply ignoring an attempt to talk entirely. Rather than changing the subject to something else, the manipulator may pretend that they don't understand what they are being asked, come up with a reason as to why it is inappropriate for them to talk about it, or insist they need more time to think their answer through. Both these tactics result in the victim's frustration at not receiving the candor they crave.

Emotional diversion is one way in which a manipulator can avoid telling the truth. For example, if the victim brings up a subject they are not comfortable talking about they may suddenly appear very sad or anxious. They may give the impression, albeit false, that there is nothing they would rather talk about but the subject is simply too painful to do so. This particular type of diversion is most commonly used on victims who are compassionate or kind people. It is not in their nature to press someone on a topic which is causing them visible distress. By manipulating the victim's emotions in this way, the manipulator is able to regain control of the situation.

Verbal diversion, also known as changing the subject, is a frequent way of avoiding the truth for manipulators. While most people change the subject from time to time, manipulators are able to do it in such a way that it is not obvious what they are doing. This prevents victims from realizing they are talking about something else entirely until it is too late.

Playing dumb is one of the most common types of evasion used by the manipulator. They will often zone in on one specific word used in a question and analyze its meaning and intention for a very long time. The victim focuses so much on explaining a particular word that they lose sight of what they originally wanted and, most probably, needed to know.

How It Occurs

A manipulator may choose to deploy diversion and evasion in a wide range of situations. What they always have in common however is the manipulator is avoiding talking about something that would make them look bad or contradict some lie they have been caught in.

A good visual metaphor for the diverter or evader is someone who runs in circles. They will expend a lot of effort moving around without ever actually going somewhere. For example, when using the evasive tactic of playing dumb, the manipulator may have about three or four points of confusion they keep returning to. When the victim responds to one, the manipulator will switch to the other, and then the next, going in conversational circles. For most people this type of circular conversation is draining, both mentally and emotionally. It is often easier to let the matter drop entirely than attempt to continue pursuing the truth.

Victims who have shown they lack the appetite for prolonged discussion are the most likely to have frequent evasion or diversion used against them. If a manipulator senses that the victim lacks the appetite for confrontation then they will use this for their own benefit. They can begin the process of diversion and evasion knowing it is only a matter of time before their victim waves the metaphorical white flag and stops attempting to put them on the spot.

How To Resist

Preventing diversion and evasion having an impact is entirely reliant upon being able to recognize they are occurring in the first place. As soon as the victim gets the sense they are being led in circles or the manipulator is changing the subject it is important to stop pursuing the information they originally sought. Why? Simply put, the manipulator is never, ever going to admit what the victim wants to know.

Some manipulators withhold information for no reason other than to see the victim in discomfort and suffering as a result of their diversion and evasion. Such manipulators are true sadists who derive pleasure from seeing someone else in pain. They cannot be fixed and will not change their ways. Therefore wasting energy on trying to help them become more honest is an utter misuse of time. Instead, the victim's focus always needs to be on escaping the situation once and for all.

Forgetting

What It Is

Manipulators are the absolute masters of having a selective memory. It is natural and human to forget things from time to time but the way in which manipulators forget is anything but natural. The best manipulators are able to forget the very things that will hurt their victim the most or cause the most mental distress and confusion.

How could forgetting something hurt a victim? In many ways, actually. Imagine confiding in someone your deepest and darkest secrets. You have opened up your heart and soul to them in a way which you have never been able to before. Then, imagine your horror when your manipulator, with an innocent facial expression and tone of voice, "forgets" something meaningful you have shared.

That time you were abused as a child? Your manipulator has no recollection of you sharing it. The name of the restaurant you shared what you thought was a very special meal? Simply not in your manipulator's recollection. The fact you are allergic to a certain food? Your manipulator has conveniently forgotten this and served it to you for the third time this month!

Of course, manipulators never really forget. In fact, quite the opposite. Manipulators are absolute experts in remembering detailed information about their victims with the sole intention of using it against them, for their own purposes, at some point in the future. In fact, ironically, remembering what to "forget" is a strength that many manipulators have!

How It Occurs

Skilled manipulators will use forgetfulness in a particularly diabolical way. There are two aspects to this psychopathy. Firstly, the manipulator will manage to appear the victim in the situation! They will make the actual victim feel guilty and embarrassed for having a problem with the manipulator's forgetfulness. After all, a bad memory is not something that people can be blamed for, right? The best manipulators know how to give an impression of being truly upset by their bad memory. The most shameless of all may even try and attribute it to something like brain damage or dementia. This means that not only is the victim criticizing the manipulator's bad memory, but also the medical condition which causes it!

The other utterly sociopathic use of forgetfulness by manipulators is to make the victim question whether they did in fact ever tell the manipulator certain things. If the manipulator is able to seem genuinely shocked at being told something then, due to the fact the manipulator holds the balance of power in the interaction, the victim will start to believe that the manipulator hasn't forgotten. Rather, they were never told! For this reason, forgetting is closely related to the previously mentioned tactics of denying reality and gaslighting.

How To Resist

Absolutely never believing a manipulator's forgetfulness is the key to resisting this tactic. Just assume every incident of a bad memory is a deliberate attempt to hurt and confuse and you are well on the way to protecting yourself from the psychological damage they are attempting to inflict.

Forgetfulness as a form of covert emotional manipulation only works if the victim seeks to check with the manipulator about something that has happened, or something they have told the manipulator. By not providing the manipulator with an opportunity to falsely forget, the victim is preventing this tactic from being used in the first place. This can be difficult to do as it is natural to seek to clarify things with people. Just always keep in mind that the manipulator is not a person in the usual sense of the word. They do not think, feel or act in normal ways. Therefore, they are not deserving of normal behavior. This may seem cold but it is an absolutely vital survival mechanism which can make the difference between the victim staying sane or losing their mental health for good.

Non Verbal Manipulation

What It Is

Most of the covert manipulation tactics explored in this book so far have involved verbal manipulation of some kind. Verbal manipulation is far from the only way in which manipulators exploit their victims, however. There are a wide range of non verbal tactics which must be recognized in order to be resisted. Some of the most common will now be explored.

Physical hypnotism is something that many manipulators are well versed in. This might sound like something from a movie but it is very real. Underestimating it is a dangerous and sometimes deadly mistake. Some manipulators are able to link an emotional state in their victim to a physical gesture. For example, at times when the victim has felt particularly comfortable and reassured by the manipulator, the manipulator may have deliberately touched the victim's shoulder. This 'anchors' the feeling to the touch. If the manipulator needs to induce this feeling of comfort and trust in the future, they are able to do so instantly, simply by replicating the physical touch. Don't believe this is possible? Either Google NLP, or think of the example of a baby. When the baby is held in a certain way, it instantly calms down. Physical hypnotism is very real indeed.

Facial expressions are another way in which a manipulator can torture their victim's emotions. A look of anger can be enough to send a worn down victim into a total and utter panic. Often, the look is enough. The manipulator needs to do nothing further. The particularly harmful aspect of this technique is that it gives the manipulator total deniability. Any victim is likely to sound crazy if they claim a facial expression caused them to break down. They will start to look like the one who is irrational and unfair.

How It Occurs

In the case of physical hypnotism, the process which makes it effective is long and drawn out. There is no way of simply linking a gesture to an emotion in an instant. Rather, it takes a prolonged period of linking the stimulus to the response. The manipulator will seek to trigger the same feelings again and again in the victim in order to be able to induce them with a gesture or touch. This lengthy aspect of the process can be beneficial for the victim as it gives them time to recognize what is taking place and resist it.

Non verbal forms of manipulation are often used when the manipulator feels their victim is especially perceptive. When a person is apt at spotting verbal manipulation, calling it out and resisting it, the manipulator may try a more subtle technique, such as physical hypnotism or manipulative facial expressions.

How To Resist
A huge red flag indicating that non verbal manipulation may have started is if the manipulator seemingly stops a verbal form of manipulation out of nowhere. This is often a sign that the manipulator has felt their words are no longer having the desired effect and have decided to try another tactic instead in the hope of eliciting a response more in line with the manipulator's desires.

It is important to note, however, that many manipulators can and will use verbal and non verbal forms of manipulation at the same time. So if you notice verbal manipulation is continuing then it does not mean that you can stop looking for the signs of non verbal manipulation. They are often used as a deadly one two punch in the manipulator's psychological arsenal. This is because looking out for either type is more than many people are capable of. Looking out for both at once is often too much for victims and therefore they are guaranteed to succumb to one form of manipulation or the other.

If you notice that a manipulative person seems to be trying to get you into the same emotional state repeatedly, such as comfort, fear or terror, it may be because they are beginning the process of physical hypnotism. Absolutely do everything within your power to avoid feeling the way the manipulator wants you to feel. If you do not fall into an emotional pattern then the manipulator will be unable to install a physical touch or expression which is able to trigger this emotion.

You will sometimes be able to notice the manipulator carrying out this type of non verbal manipulation on other people before they do it to you. If this happens, consider yourself lucky. Most manipulators will be sure to keep their cards very close to their chest and never give away any of their tactics in a way which can warn a victim of what is to come. If you notice any signs of non verbal manipulation, be extra vigilant of it being applied to you. And, more importantly, start figuring out how to get the manipulator out of your life for good.

Pavlovian Conditioning

What It Is

Have you heard of Pavlov's famous experiment? It involved playing a sound every time dogs were presented with a piece of meat to eat. This happened for a prolonged period. Eventually, the experimenters were able to induce the reaction of salivation at the sound alone without the stimulus of the food being present.

What this experiment shows is that living creatures can be conditioned. You think humans are immune from this? Far from it! Do you ever hear the jingle of your favorite product and instantly get a craving for that product? How about seeing someone else yawn and suddenly find yourself yawning as well? What about driving? At first every little motion is a struggle that needs to be consciously carried out. After a while though your body will respond to what it sees on the road and make the motions involuntarily.

So how do manipulators use Pavlovian Conditioning for their own evil purposes? They manage to link emotional states such as terror, fear and panic to sensory stimulus. Therapists have countless tales of women who will have a full panic attack if they hear the sound of a car pulling into a driveway. This is because, in the past, they would have been in an emotionally and physically manipulative relationship which involved violence that always followed the sound of a car arriving home.

Another example of Pavlovian conditioning in the context of a manipulative relationship is the smell of aftershave. If a woman has been around a man who wears a particular scent then smelling it, even years later, can cause the woman to feel irrational terror and panic. This is due to the fact that scent, in particular, is linked to the parts of the brain which deal with memory and emotion.

How It Occurs

So how do manipulators use Pavlovian conditioning for their own purposes? In a number of different ways. Firstly, some especially twisted manipulators may play a certain song or type of music when they act in a certain way towards a victim. For example, a particular type of classical music every time they behave aggressively, perhaps some jazz when they offer false comfort. After a prolonged period of this, the manipulator can trigger the emotional response just by playing the music and doing nothing else.

Some manipulators take this a step further and offer contrasting stimulus in quick succession. For example, manipulators will offer one stimulus that makes a victim feel panic, followed by one that causes comfort, followed by another which causes fear. The victim will feel a rapid range of emotions with no discernible cause. The manipulator can then either act as the savior by providing some kind of comfort to their victim, or use their scrambled emotional state as a time of carrying out yet another emotionally manipulative tactic.

How To Resist
Understanding the process is the first step in avoiding becoming conditioned in this way. If

you know how it works, you know how to prevent it. Some of the most common things to look out for include the same music being played again and again or some other type of repeated pattern such as slamming a door or wearing a certain item of clothing.

If, as a victim, you notice some kind of repeated behavior occurring, do everything in your power to disrupt the pattern. So change the song, look away from anything visual the manipulator is doing, whatever it takes.

Also, refuse to be led emotionally by the manipulator. If they try and comfort you, remain ice cold inside. If they try and scare you, stay brave. They are relying on you feeling a set range of emotions when promoted. If you effectively manage to avoid either the desired emotional state or the trigger they are hoping to link to it then you can avoid becoming Pavlovian conditioned.

Find Your Escape

You now know all of the main tactics manipulators use to covertly impact your emotions. Being forewarned is to be forearmed. You know how to resist their efforts and how to stop them from gaining additional power over yourself.

This alone is not enough however. Think of all of the above measures as a temporary fix. A way to stop the flames from spreading long enough to get far away from the burning house.

Make no mistake, emotional abuse will continue. And it can kill. Over three women die every single day in America from an abusive relationship. Countless more suffer to the point they are driven crazy.

You will only be able to resist a covert emotional manipulator for so long. Eventually, they will find something that breaks you.

I know you might be confused. You might feel compassion and want to help them. You might believe they can change.

Sadly, they will never change. If you value your life, your only answer is to get out.

Escaping this kind of scenario is not easy. And trying to escape it the wrong way can even be more dangerous than staying. But escape is your only answer.

Read on to discover the different escape routes you can take to get away from a covert emotional manipulator once and for all.

You will learn what to do and what not to do.

Your path to freedom, happiness and an independent life lies ahead. Please read on. It is your only chance to regain control of your freedom and make your emotions your own once more.

Chapter 8 - Escape or Die

The title of this chapter may sound a little dramatic. Die? Are you really guaranteed to die if you do not escape a manipulative situation? Actually, yes.

You may not die in the sense that your life will end, although that is definitely a very real possibility. But your freedom is sure to die. Your happiness will die. Your sanity will die. Basically, you will suffer a fate that is worse than death. If you were actually dead, you would be at peace. You would not have to suffer the endless misery that comes with being stuck in a manipulative situation. Instead, your body lives, but your spirit does not. You are trapped in an invisible prison, forced to suffer each day without the promise of ever getting free.

Of course, literal death is a tragic but very real possibility as well. At least three women each day are killed in the USA as a result of being in an abusive relationship. Countless more choose to end their own lives as it is the only escape from their torment that their broken mind allows them to see.

It doesn't have to come to this. There are several ways that you can retake your freedom and live the life of happiness that you deserve. Is escaping easy? No. Is it worth it? Absolutely. Your choice is none other than that of freedom or a slow, miserable, spiritual and emotional death.

A strong word of caution must be emphasized before we begin to share the ways to escape a manipulative situation. Manipulative people are dangerous and devious. They will often stop at nothing to regain control of a situation. For such people, their victim escaping their clutches represents the ultimate loss of control. Many manipulators will stop at absolutely nothing to restore things to the way they want. If they find out that this is not possible they may resort to acts of violence, stalking and other forms of extremely dangerous, criminal behavior.

That is not to say that these people cannot be escaped from. Quite the opposite. Thousands of people each year find the courage and strength to take their life back. By following the advice of this chapter you will be able to experience the joy of your own escape without running the risks that come with escaping in the wrong way.

Before The Escape - Failing to Plan is Planning to Fail

The exact nature of your escape from a manipulative person, and situation, depends heavily upon the type of manipulator you find yourself with and the details of the situation. One thing that every escape has in common, however, is the need to plan very carefully before carrying it out. A well planned escape makes all the difference between success and failure. Also, more importantly, planning makes the difference between danger and safety. So let's discover how to plan properly.

The first thing to realize when planning an escape is that very few people must know about it beforehand. People have a way of being unable to keep secrets or giving away the wrong information to the wrong person. Even if you tell people and they have your best intentions in mind they may accidently let the wrong thing slip at the wrong time.

There is also another key reason for telling as few people as possible about what you have planned. Many manipulators do not respect personal boundaries in any way whatsoever. They may go through your phone, your email and your social media on a regular basis without you having any idea. If they discover what you are planning then you are placing yourself in a position of immense physical danger.

Even if you think that your manipulator is not going through your phone or your social media and that you have covered your tracks by deleting messages, there is no way that you can be sure. Did you know that software exists which can be discretely installed on a PC or phone and allows someone to spy on you in real time? As you are typing, each and every button you press could be being transmitted directly to your manipulator. There is no way you would know this is happening and therefore there is no clear way to protect against it.

That is not to say that you should not tell anyone what you are planning. Rather, it is important to tell one trusted person only. This could be a best friend or a member of your family. It is absolutely vital that you trust this person with your life as this is effectively what is at stake. You need to know this person will not let anything slip, even accidently. The reason for telling them is so that firstly, they can support you through the process in any way you need and secondly, so

that if anything goes wrong they are able to
inform the police what has happened and who is
responsible.

Choosing the right person to let know what you
are up to is only the first stage of the planning
process. It is also absolutely vital to choose a
physical place you can escape to and spend some
time in the aftermath of your escape. This,
ideally, will be somewhere out of town,
preferably as far away as possible. This is due to
the fact that the manipulator is likely to look
everywhere they can think of in the aftermath of
you escaping the situation. The place you choose
should be far away geographically and also
somewhere that the manipulator will not be able
to figure out easily.

Preparing financially for life without the
manipulator is another key aspect of planning.
This can be very difficult as some types of
manipulators are incredibly controlling when it
comes to finances. Ideally, you will have one to

two months expenses saved up and be able to access them in a way which will not arouse suspicion. If this is not possible then your one trusted friend or family member should be asked to help you out. You will be able to repay them after you have got clear of the situation. This is just a temporary measure.

If you are in a situation where you are living with your manipulator, and you want to move out, planning to take the things you need with you is important but difficult. Anything that is replaceable should be left behind. Only absolutely essential things like valuable jewelry, identity documents and other similar things should be taken. Ideally, you should only take as many things as you can fit into one bag. This makes the practical side of the escape much easier.

In the time period leading up to your escape you should put together a duffel bag or similar sized bag of new purchases from outside of the home.

For example, you should pack some underwear, clothes, toiletries and other similar items. They should not be taken from the home as their absence would likely arouse suspicion. Instead, they should all be new purchases. When you have carefully put together your bag it is vital to find a safe place to store it. Some good ideas for such places include with your one trusted person or at some kind of rental locker space, such as a gym locker.

The above steps are the basic essentials you need to consider when planning your escape from a manipulative situation. There may be other steps you need to consider in light of your particular scenario or some of the above ideas may not apply. If you are sure to follow the advice though then you are putting yourself in a position of preparedness and safety ahead of your escape.

Now that you have made practical preparations for your escape, it's time to plan the escape itself.

Planning The Actual Escape

The preceding section of this chapter gave you all of the information you need to make some preparations ahead of your escape. While essential, it is not enough. Equally, if not more important, is to plan the actual escape. This includes the nature of the escape, the timing of the escape and what you will do if something goes wrong. Having a clear plan in mind for the time period after the escape is also essential. This is because after the escape is often the most dangerous time as the manipulator will know what has happened and will be looking for revenge.

The first key step in this process is understanding exactly what an escape means to you. Every situation is different and not all of them require a dramatic escape which involves hiding out in some remote location. We will now look at some of the more appropriate escape methods depending on the type of manipulative situation you are trying to get away from.

If you are with one of the more serious types of relationship manipulator, such as someone who is violent, or gaslighting, or denying reality then it is absolutely vital to put physical distance between yourself and your manipulator. This is because these types of manipulators are the ones who will cross the line into violence and even murder if they are provoked. This is the most serious type of manipulative situation you can find yourself in so make sure to leave nothing to chance when attempting to escape it.

Some types of relationship manipulators are less dangerous but you still should err on the side of caution. For example, if the person you are with manipulates you through lying and minimizing then you may not need to plan such a dramatic and comprehensive escape from this type of scenario. It may be enough to break up with such a person from a distance and make sure they know you will go to the police if they attempt to remain in contact with you.

Other types of situations requires a different approach. If you are stuck in a manipulative workplace situation then you may find that changing jobs is the only way that you can get out. It may be tempting to quit in the heat of the moment but this is the wrong way to go about it. It is absolutely vital to have another job, known as a parachute job, lined up before you quit. Otherwise, you will face serious financial trouble after quitting the manipulative situation. Schedule interviews for days off from the office and consider using vacation time to book all your new job interviews into a two week time period. This can allow for the job search process to be less stressful for you.

Escaping a manipulative family situation can be the most difficult escape of all. This is due to the fact that we remain a member of our family for our whole lifetime. It is not like a job or a relationship where we can simply quit the scenario and walk away from it. If you are dealing with a manipulative family situation the most probable first route of escape is to try and draw clear boundaries between yourself and the person who is manipulating you. For example, if you find yourself being the financial provider for a member of your family, absolutely cut off all financial support to them. Make it clear what you are doing and why you are doing it. Sometimes, this is not enough. Sadly, some families cannot be fixed, and as painful as it is, you may need to stop attending family events. Only you can make this choice and it should not be made lightly.

The Escape Itself

Once you have made both practical preparations for the escape and settled upon the time of escape that is most appropriate for your situation it is time to execute your plan and begin your new life as a free person. We will now look at some advice relating to how to conduct your actual escape in the most proper way possible.

If you are escaping one of the most dangerous types of manipulator, such as a gaslighter or violent abuser, then you need to be extra vigilant during your escape. Plan the actual time of escape from your shared home when you absolutely know for certain the manipulator will not be at home. This should ideally be during the middle of a work day when you know they are actually at work. It can be worth calling the workplace using a false identity, such as a parcel company, in order to make sure they are physically at work. If they were to come home during your escape it could be an incredibly dangerous situation for you.

You need to gather up your vital bag of essential documents and other items, as discussed in an earlier section of this chapter. It is also worth leaving a letter for the manipulator. This should be calm, brief and to the point. A sample letter you may wish to use, or base your own letter on, is provided below.

"I have chosen to leave this home. You are forbidden to contact me or make any effort at all to get in touch. The police have been informed of what is taking place and will be called right away if you attempt to go against my wishes."

Avoid the temptation to go into reasons for what you are doing or to blame the manipulator. None of this will work and is only likely to anger them or provoke them into doing something violent. It is important to note that, at the time you write the letter, you will not have actually been in touch with the police. This is because it is vital you get out of the situation and into a safe place before you attempt to do so. Advice on the right time, and way, to involve the police will be provided shortly.

Once you have gathered up your bag of vital items and left the note for your manipulator, it is time to contact your trusted person on the outside. Tell them you are going ahead with your plan. They may come and pick you up or you may arrange to meet them somewhere. The important thing is you get to them as soon as possible. This is because a manipulator will often have a very intense level of hesitation with regards to acting manipulatively around another person. The other person represents an unknown factor that the manipulator cannot control. Therefore, they are one of the key elements protecting your safety.

If you have followed the steps in the earlier planning section of this chapter then you will already have a safe place lined up that you can stay in for awhile. Get to this place as soon as possible. Ideally, your trusted friend or family member should be able to stay with you for the first day or so until you get accustomed to being away from the manipulative person or situation. Once you have reached your place of safety there are a few things to keep in mind.

Firstly, depending on the severity of the manipulative situation and the person who was manipulating you, it might be a vital step to contact the police preemptively. Explain that you have been through a certain situation and have escaped it. This will inform the police so that if the manipulator tries to get in contact with you again they are prepared to arrest him or her having known the full details of the background to the story. It can also give you priceless peace of mind knowing that a powerful entity such as the police will be looking out for you.

Secondly, you need to make sure your mental state is correct following your escape. It can be very confusing in the time following the escape of a manipulative situation and you may find some of your thoughts surprising. Some common feelings include guilt for escaping the situation and the desire to return to it. Resist this at all costs. Realize that you did the right thing in escaping and you are better off this way.

Understand that the way you are feeling is simply the lingering effects of the dependency and vulnerability that the manipulator instilled in you over the period of their manipulation.

After The Escape

Perhaps the most important part of the escape is what happens after it has occurred. Many people mistakenly think that their work is done as soon as they are out of the manipulative situation. This is an understandable belief but not one which is true. In actual fact there is a lot that is still to be done after the escape has been completed. Failing to act in the proper way after the escape can lead to the victim feeling bad and returning to the manipulative situation. Or, even worse, finding herself entering into another manipulative situation soon after escaping the first one! By following the advice in this section of the book the victim can help to ensure they do not end up making the same mistakes again.

The first and perhaps most important step is safety. Make sure that, if the manipulator tries to contact you again, the police are informed right away. It is important to discretely inform someone trusted at your place of work or study of the situation you find yourself in, so that if the manipulator should show up unannounced, they know what to do. You may want to look into the laws regarding self defense in your particular city and region. Carrying something like pepper spray or a rape alarm can help you feel secure and safe and regain the confidence you need to go about your life.

Once you have taken every step possible to ensure your safety it is vital to start rebuilding your life. Many people who have escaped manipulative situations return to them because they are all they have ever known. Getting out of the situation leaves a void in the person's life which they attempt to fill in the wrong way. Therefore knowing how to fill the void in the right way is a key part of moving on from a manipulation.

Entering into a romantic relationship of any kind too soon is an absolute mistake to be avoided. After a serious emotional manipulation a person needs time to rediscover who they are and how they feel about things away from the emotional control that they have found themselves in prior to their escape. Even if the person you are thinking of becoming romantic with seems like a good person there is always a chance you have subconsciously sought out another manipulator. There is no exact rule of how long to avoid a romantic situation for but a month to six weeks at absolute minimum seems to be a good general guideline. Trust your heart and the advice of your close friends with regards to this.

Another key mistake to avoid is starting to use drugs or alcohol particularly heavily following escaping from an emotional manipulation. Just like romance, intoxicants can sometimes be used as a substitute for the manipulator. You used to be dependent upon the manipulator so you transfer that dependency to a bottle instead. Don't do this! Staying strong and healthy, both physically and mentally, is a key component of manipulation recovery.

Checking up on the manipulator is strangely tempting but must be avoided at all costs. Many victims have an urge to see 'how their manipulator is doing' out of simple curiosity. Just avoid this. By doing this you open yourself up to the possibility of being manipulated into thinking the person has changed and giving them another chance. In the worst case scenario you risk being hurt or even killed. Avoid going to places you used to go to together or contacting mutual friends in any way. A clean break is absolutely vital in order for you to move on with your life.

So you know what not to do, so what should you do? Well, enjoy your freedom! Begin to rediscover who YOU are and what YOU love doing. Here are some ideas to make the most of this beautiful opportunity.

Making the Most of Your Freedom

Physical exercise is a key part of ensuring you stay strong and healthy following an escape from an emotional manipulator. It has been proven that exercise helps to protect against conditions such as depression and anxiety. You will be at perhaps the most raw and vulnerable state of your life in the time period after escaping a manipulator. By exercising you are helping to both protect your psyche, strengthen your body and also add evidence to your new self-image as a strong and independent person.

The type of exercise you choose doesn't matter as long as it is something you enjoy. Maybe your manipulator used to be very controlling and didn't allow you to go to the gym or to exercise classes. If this was the case then enjoy the newfound opportunity! Do something you always wanted to do but never had the chance to before. By doing this you are reinforcing in your mind that you are better off without the manipulator and able to live a happy and full life without them.

Reconnecting with old friends and making new friends is another important part of moving on after your escape. It is very likely that your manipulator tried to restrict or cut off entirely the type of people you spoke to while you were being manipulated by them. It is important that you realize you are now free to speak to and be friends with whoever you want. Reaching out to old friends is a great way to make the most of this newfound freedom. You may or may not want to tell them what has happened to you depending on how close you are to them and how you think they would react to the information. Just remember that you are now in control and you are free to tell anyone anything you like.

Spirituality and religion can also play an important part in your life after your manipulator. If you follow a particular religious belief system then make the most of its wisdom and the strength it can provide you with. By becoming involved in life at a church or other faith organization you will have a routine and be surrounded by positive and supportive people. If you are not a member of an organized religion this is no problem. Read poetry and listen to music you find gives you comfort and reassurance. Anything you can do to boost your spirit and mind is incredibly valuable at this time of your life.

When They Won't Go Away

Tragically, many manipulators will not go quietly. You can do absolutely everything right but it does not guarantee that you will be left alone to live your life in peace. This section of the book offers insight into some of the most common ways that a manipulator tries to get back in touch and offers advice on how to protect yourself from such situations.

Sometimes the manipulator will try to get back in touch with you directly, either in person or via messaging or social media. If they do they will usually try one of two tactics to win you back. The first approach is to try and elicit sympathy from you. They will claim that they are nothing without you, that they cannot live without you and that they will make any changes they need to get you back into their life. Avoid this at all costs. Don't believe them. It is human nature to want a happy ending and the romantic or compassionate side of many people's personalities will trick them into being tempted to go along with such stories. Do not give in, no matter what is said.

The other main approach that a manipulator might use is seeking to threaten or strong arm you into becoming a part of their life once again.

They may threaten to harm or hurt you if you don't go along with their wishes. They may threaten to ruin your life or to hurt members of your family. This may be incredibly upsetting and distressing to hear but it is important to stay strong and avoid listening. Most manipulators will not go through with their threats. A small minority will. This is why it is absolutely vital to contact the police should a manipulator get back in touch with you. Police in the modern day and age are well trained in how to deal with these situations and can offer you protection and reassurance.

Aside from trying to get back in touch with you directly, many manipulators will try and do so indirectly. They may try to use mutual friends to speak on their behalf. If this occurs, calmly explain to the third party that you are not prepared to speak to the manipulator under any circumstance whatsoever. You don't have to explain why if you don't want to. Ask the third person to not speak to you about your manipulator again, ever. And explain if they do so you will have no option but to cut that person out of your life as well. Most third parties will respect your wishes as they will have had no idea at all of how serious the situation was.

Chapter 9: Learning Your Lesson

It is a tragic fact of life that we are doomed to repeat the mistakes of our past. At least, it can seem that way sometimes. How many people do you know who get into the wrong kinds of relationships over and over again? How many people do you know who manage to get free of a job that was stifling their soul only to see them sleepwalk into another right away? Thankfully, we are not slaves to our past. We can make a clean break and make better choices moving forward. This is not easy and requires honesty and the ability to self-examine and learn. We will now explore exactly how to learn lessons following a manipulation and avoid returning to similar situations in the future.

One of the keys to understanding a manipulation is not trying to rush the process. After escaping a manipulative situation you will need some time and space to recover from what has happened. Trying to analyze the situation too soon will lead only to disappointment and defeat. Instead, wait until the rawest of wounds from the manipulation have healed. Then, and only then, should you begin the process of trying to understand what has happened to you.

So, where to start? At the beginning! You need to think back carefully and clearly to the time before the manipulation began. What was your life like? How did you feel? How did you spend your time? Were you happy or sad? If you need to, speak to people who were close to you in your life at that time. Sometimes, getting the perspective of an outsider is the best way to understand what was going on.

When you identify the mentality that led you into becoming involved with a manipulative person and situation you can ensure that you work on these aspects of your character. As the old saying goes, 'prevention is better than cure'. By preventing yourself falling into the same state of mind as you were in before the manipulation you can proactively ensure you avoid this trap in the future.

It is also important to look back throughout your life and identify any common themes. Perhaps you often end up with someone who lies. Perhaps you often seem to fall for people who use empty words. By identifying your own personal vulnerabilities you can ensure that if you notice yourself going down that destructive road again in the future you stop yourself before it is too late.

Letting a friend know about your analysis is also valuable. This way, they can let you know if they notice you making the same mistakes again. It is better to have an ally in these situations than to feel alone.

Chapter 10: Conclusion - Final Thoughts

By this point you are equipped with an understanding of what covert manipulation is. You know the types of situations in which manipulation can occur and the types of people who are likely to use it. You also know the specific tactics used and how to resist them. Most importantly, you know how to escape a bad situation and rebuild your life.

It is important you feel a deep sense of hope. No matter how bad a situation may seem, there is always a way out. There is light at the end of every tunnel even if you can't see it at the time.

If you ever find yourself in a bad situation you now have the complete understanding of how to recognize it, how to deal with it and how to move on from it.

Please also be aware that friends may be experiencing the same problems. If you know someone who is troubled by being stuck in a manipulative life situation you are now equipped with the knowledge you need to ensure they are safe and secure.

The most important thing to remember is that manipulators only have as much power as we give them. They cannot force their way into our lives, hearts and minds. If we stay strong and vigilant against their danger then we can protect ourselves from getting hurt.

Most people in the world are good. Don't become excessively paranoid about manipulators. They do exist, and they are evil, but they are not everywhere.

Use this information wisely. Help yourself and help others. The more that we fight back against manipulators, the more we show them they will not be allowed to do as they please and ruin innocent lives.

44965330R00143

Made in the USA
San Bernardino, CA
28 January 2017